D0926494

Praise for
Seven Trends in Corporate Training and Development

"With his extensive background, knowledge, and experience on the subject of training and development, it is no surprise that Ibraiz Tarique has written a book that marries T&D theory and practice to the new ways we learn today. Ibraiz brings a discerning eye to emerging trends and reveals how to leverage them into successful programs. *Seven Trends in Corporate Training and Development* should be on the bookshelf of every training and development professional—and those aspiring to become one."

—**Ellen Weisbord**, Professor, Academic Director Executive MBA Program, Lubin School of Business, Pace University, New York

"In his book *Seven Trends in Corporate Training and Development*, Dr. Ibraiz Tarique examines the importance of the intrinsic learning capability of individuals, as well as the extrinsic environments in which they perform. His multidimensional approach to learning offers insights that can be used to examine the influences of individual development. The understanding and consideration of both dimensions transforms the way in which programs are not only designed, but even more importantly, how they should be supported as students are tasked with leveraging new skills and knowledge they have learned in the classroom. This book is a must-read for any professional involved in workplace training and development."

—**Lindamarie Werntz Coatman**, Human Resources Executive

Seven Trends in Corporate Training and Development

Strategies to Align Goals with Employee Needs

Ibraiz Tarique, Ph.D.

Associate Publisher: Amy Neidlinger
Executive Editor: Jeanne Glasser Levine
Operations Specialist: Jodi Kemper
Cover Designer: Chuti Prasertsith
Managing Editor: Kristy Hart
Senior Project Editor: Lori Lyons
Copy Editor: Karen Annett
Proofreader: Apostrophe Editing Services
Indexer: Lisa Stumpf
Senior Compositor: Gloria Schurick
Manufacturing Buyer: Dan Uhrig

© 2014 by Ibraiz Tarique, Ph.D.
Pearson Education, Inc.
Upper Saddle River, New Jersey 07458

For information about buying this title in bulk quantities, or for special sales opportunities (which may include electronic versions; custom cover designs; and content particular to your business, training goals, marketing focus, or branding interests), please contact our corporate sales department at corpsales@pearsoned.com or (800) 382-3419.

For government sales inquiries, please contact governmentsales@pearsoned.com.

For questions about sales outside the U.S., please contact international@pearsoned.com.

Printed in the United States of America

First Printing May 2014

ISBN-10: 0-13-313888-7
ISBN-13: 978-0-13-313888-7

Pearson Education LTD.
Pearson Education Australia PTY, Limited.
Pearson Education Singapore, Pte. Ltd.
Pearson Education Asia, Ltd.
Pearson Education Canada, Ltd.
Pearson Educación de Mexico, S.A. de C.V.
Pearson Education—Japan
Pearson Education Malaysia, Pte. Ltd.

Library of Congress Control Number: 2014933123

This book is dedicated to my father, Asif Tarique,
who is my role model, source of my wisdom,
and whom I love very much.

Contents-at-a-Glance

Contents

Acknowledgments

Several individuals have helped to make this book a reality. A *special thanks* to my family for their unwavering support. A special gratitude goes to my wife. Without you, this book would not be possible! You provided the strength, courage, and encouragement to keep going, and time and time again you made me realize that this is all worth the time and effort. I thank my parents for teaching me the importance of learning, intellectual curiosity, and instilling in me an appreciation for the value of education and a desire for continuous pursuit of knowledge.

I am indebted to Dr. Paula Caligiuri for providing the opportunity to write this book. Thank you for inspiring and motivating me to keep working on this book. You helped me at various points on this journey, for which I'm very appreciative. I am thankful to Jeanne Levine, who gave me the support and guidance necessary to complete this book. Thanks also go to Lori Lyons and Karen Arnett for their help with the editing and production of the book.

In addition, I am thankful to all the individuals who helped me in the research for this book: Emily Cheng, Tamara Kelly, and Sasha Pustovit. I would like to thank the Lubin School of Business, Pace University, and my excellent colleagues for supporting my interests in human resource management. Finally, I would like to thank my students (both current and past) who continuously inspire me and remind me every day that learning is a lifelong process.

About the Author

Ibraiz Tarique, Ph.D., is an Associate Professor of Human Resources Management and Director of Global HRM Programs at the Lubin School of Business, Pace University, New York City Campus. He earned his Ph.D. in Industrial Relations and Human Resource Management from Rutgers University (2005). Dr. Tarique publishes and consults in the area of international human resource management. His academic research interest is in international human resource management with a focus on issues related to global talent management and investments in human capital. His applied research focuses on examining the approaches that organizations use to develop HR and global HR professionals.

He has written extensively in academic and professional journals. His publications include articles in the *International Journal of Human Resource Management*, *Journal of World Business*, *Human Resource Management Review*, and *International Journal of Training and Development*, in addition to chapters contributed to several books. He has presented numerous papers at the Annual Academy of Management Meetings. He is a member of several editorial boards of the international peer-reviewed journals, including *International Journal of Human Resource Management*, *International Journal of Training and Development*, *Journal of Global Mobility*, *European Journal of International Management*, and *Cross Cultural Management: An International Journal*.

His coauthored paper on Global Talent Management (with Dr. Randall Schuler) in the *Journal of World Business* was ranked as one of the most downloaded and cited paper in 2012 and 2013 by the publication. In addition, his coauthored paper on Global Leadership Effectiveness (with Dr. Paula Caligiuri) was published in the *Journal of World Business* and was awarded (with Dr. Paula Caligiuri) the

Best Global Leadership Research published in 2013 by the Global Leadership Advancement Center.

Dr. Tarique is the coauthor of *International Human Resource Management: Policies and Practices for Multinational Enterprises*, a comprehensive textbook that provides a foundation for understanding the theory and practice of international human resource management. He is also the coauthor of *Strategic Talent Management: Contemporary Issues in International Context*. This book examines the topical issue of talent management from a strategic perspective.

Dr. Tarique teaches HRM courses at four levels: executive MBA, regular MBA, MSc in HRM, and undergraduate HRM.

Preface

The trends that influence workplace training and development are changing in significant ways:

- The *knowledge economy* is growing and becoming an inevitable part of the modern business structure.
- Jobs are becoming more fluid and specialized.
- Knowledge turnover is now rapid and becoming a new reality.
- The aging of the workforce is creating a need to develop new sources of talent.
- The proliferation and access of knowledge on the Internet have given rise to the greater demand for the ability to discern fact from opinion.

These trends, among others, are changing the way people learn and making investments in employee training and development more critical in determining the success of an organization than it has been in the past.

This book provides insights into the challenges arising from the top seven most significant trends affecting training and development today, offering tangible suggestions for practice to address those trends.

The motive for writing this book was to provide a simple, easy-to-read coverage of the seven trends affecting training and development. The concepts, ideas, and suggestions offered in this book provide a clear picture of the challenges facing the training and development function and the type of training and development practices that are needed to develop today's employees.

This book is divided into three parts. Part I, "The Changing Context," includes three chapters and sets the scene for the seven trends. Chapter 1, "Forces Shaping the Corporate Learning Function," describes forces such as globalization, workforce demographics, changing job structures, and hybrid career paths. Chapter 2, "Adult Learning and Development," covers important definitions and terminology. Chapter 3, "The Art of Knowledge Acquisition," describes the various types and levels of knowledge (for example, tacit versus explicit) and the various ways adults search for information and why these information-seeking skills are as important as learning.

Part II, "Emerging Trends in Training and Development Practices," describes the seven most significant trends affecting training and development today. This part includes seven chapters (Chapters 4–10). Chapter 4, "Technology-Based Learning," discusses the first trend. This chapter discusses how technology influences knowledge acquisition, access to information, learning styles, and various methods of delivering and sharing instructional content. Chapter 5, "Informal Learning," examines the second trend. This chapter examines the importance of informal learning in contemporary organizations and explains why this form of unsystematic and unstructured type of learning is becoming popular. Chapter 6, "Customized Learning and Learner Control," focuses on the third trend. It describes customized learning, what customized learning is, the importance of customized learning, and how learner control is related to customized learning. Chapter 7, "Continuous Learning," describes the fourth trend. It discusses the importance of continuous learning in organizations and describes why this type of learning is becoming popular. Chapter 8, "Learning and Development Through Teamwork," concentrates on the fifth trend. It discusses how teams work, the traits that make team members effective, and the importance of collaborative learning. Chapter 9, "Extreme Development: Stretch Assignments and Learning Agility," examines the sixth trend. This chapter describes the importance of work experiences that contain *stretch* and how stretch assignments are one of the best ways to develop critical thinking, which has become the new imperative. The chapter then describes the concept of learning agility and discusses why the concept is important to employee development. Chapter 10, "The New Experts," examines the seventh and final trend. This chapter describes what expertise is and how it is developed and maintained in the context of new changes in the business environment.

Finally, Part III, "Strategic Directions for Training and Development," includes two chapters. Chapter 11, "Investment in Workforce Learning and Development," describes why it is important to view employee training and development in terms of investments, the different kinds of investments, and the various methods to evaluate the effectiveness of investments in human capital. Chapter 12, "The Future of Training and Development," provides perspectives on the field, its progress, its prospects, and possibilities for the future.

You will notice that the chapters vary in length and scope. A major reason for this variation is the development of the specific field and the level of complexity in each area.

This book can be used in a variety of ways. This book can be used by human resources management professionals involved in training and development of employees, with positions such as trainer, director of learning and development, director of talent management, chief learning officer, and HR training manager.

This book can also be used as the main text in college courses that focus on training and development and as a supplement to a traditional introductory course in human resources management.

Part I

The Changing Context

1

Forces Shaping the Corporate Learning Function

What's in this chapter:

- The corporate learning function
- Globalization: global workplace and a borderless workforce
- Talent management: a surplus of workers and a shortage of required competencies
- Workforce segmentation: various employee groups
- Careers: hybrid careers and fluid jobs
- Learning technologies: continue to evolve

The learning and development industry in the United States is a multibillion dollar industry.[1] Successful organizations use the learning function to increase efficiency and improve their competitiveness. Organizations that focus on learning share certain characteristics, such as having a corporate culture of learning, a commitment to employee development, a strong belief that performance can be improved through learning and development, and a continued investment in training to ensure a supply of a fully qualified workforce for the future. Examples of such organizations include UPS, Verizon, and Hilton Worldwide.[2]

The Corporate Learning Function

Human resources management refers to a set of policies and practices that an organization uses to manage its workforce. The *corporate learning function* is part of the human resources management that is responsible for making sure that employees have the competencies that are required for successful job completion. *Competencies* refer to the combination of knowledge, skills, abilities, attitudes, and behaviors. More specifically, the corporate learning function is responsible for the instruction, maintenance, application, and transfer of competencies.

- **Instruction:** This refers to providing employees with needed competencies to perform their jobs successfully while supporting the organization's goals and strategy.
- **Maintenance:** This refers to helping employees preserve learned competencies.
- **Application:** This refers to helping employees continuously put to use learned competencies in the job environment.
- **Transfer:** This refers to the transfer of competencies from one person to another, from one person to a group, from one group to another, and so on.

The mechanisms or tools that organizations use to instruct, maintain, apply, and transfer competencies are called *training* and *development* activities. Training activities focus more on solving short-term performance concerns; that is, training provides competencies employees need in their current jobs. Developmental activities, in contrast, focus on competencies necessary to fulfill a strategic need in the future. Table 1.1 provides examples of training and development activities.

Table 1.1 Examples of Training and Development Activities[3]

Examples of Training Activities	Examples of Developmental Activities
• Diversity training	• Rotational developmental programs
• Safety training	• Global teams
• Sexual harassment training	• Graduate or executive-level university coursework
• Computer training	• Mentoring and/or coaching
• Team training	• Workshops, seminars, and conferences
	• Stretch assignments

The corporate learning industry is going through rapid change, growth, and development. Today, more than ever before, there are many forces affecting the corporate learning landscape. These forces are generating intense pressure on organizations to keep pace with a set of new norms for managing the learning function. Specific forces impacting the corporate learning landscape are discussed next.

Globalization: Global Workplace and a Borderless Workforce

Most organizations, large and small, are involved in some form of international business activities. Larger organizations such as multinational enterprises like Apple, Inc., and nongovernmental organizations (NGOs) like the United Nations have affiliates in various regions and countries that employ people from a variety of cultural and ethnic backgrounds.[4] Table 1.2 provides a snapshot of the extent of globalization in the United States.

Table 1.2 Extent of Globalization in the United States

Employment by U.S. and Foreign Multinational Corporations (MNCs)[5]

- 34.5 million workers are employed worldwide by U.S. multinational companies.
- 22.9 million workers are employed by U.S. parent companies in the United States.
- 11.7 million workers are employed abroad by majority-owned foreign affiliates of U.S. MNCs.
- 5.6 million workers are employed in the United States by majority-owned U.S. affiliates of foreign MNCs.

Import and Export Trends[6]

- 83,050 companies both export and import goods.
- 219,210 companies only export goods.
- 100,910 companies only import goods.

Labor Force Characteristics of Foreign-Born Workers[7]

- The U.S. labor force includes 25.0 million foreign-born persons. They represent 16.1% of the total labor force.
- 48.3% of the foreign-born labor force is composed of Hispanics; 23.7% of the foreign-born labor force is composed of Asians.

Languages Spoken in America[8]

- 60.6 million people (age 5 and over) speak a language other than English at home.
- Examples of languages include Spanish (37.6 million), Chinese (2.9 million), Tagalog (1.6 million), Vietnamese (1.4 million), French (1.3 million), German (1.1 million), and Korean (1.1 million).

Source: U.S. Department of Commerce, Bureau of Economic Analysis, U.S. Department of Commerce, United States Census Bureau, Bureau of Labor Statistics, U.S. Department of Labor, U.S. Department of Commerce, Economics and Statistics Administration

As Table 1.2 indicates, for most U.S. companies and for most international organizations, involvement in international labor and product markets is likely to grow rapidly in the coming years. As organizations increase their international activities, they face two important challenges:

- **Managing a global workplace:** A *global workplace* consists of individuals from a variety of cultural, geographic, and racial backgrounds who interact and collaborate with one other.

- **Managing a borderless workforce:** A *borderless workforce* includes individuals who have international job responsibilities and are dispersed geographically, virtually, and across countries and regions.

In a global workplace with a borderless workforce, cross-cultural and ethnic differences can influence how individuals interact with one another, approach differences and conflicts, and solve problems. Misunderstandings and miscommunication are unavoidable. The learning function has the responsibility of providing *cross-cultural competencies* that enable individuals to understand cross-cultural differences as well as appreciate the characteristics and benefits of multicultural and multilingual diversity that exist in a global workplace with a borderless workforce.

Types of Cross-Cultural Competencies. Cross-cultural competencies can be cultural-general,[9] cultural-specific,[10] region-specific, and megacities-specific:

- Cultural-general competencies provide an understanding of how countries and cultures differ in general and the impact of these differences on individual behavior. Examples include the general dimensions on which most cultures differ such as individualism versus collectivism, power distance, masculinity versus femininity, uncertainty avoidance, and long-term versus short-term orientation.[11]

- Cultural-specific competencies provide an understanding of a specific country or culture, such as a country's language, customs, diversity, history, and geography. In addition, cultural-specific competencies provide language skills.
- Region-specific competencies focus on how and why organizations strategically view particular countries such as those represented in the Organization of Economic Cooperation and Development (OECD), the European Union, the Association of South-East Asian Nations, and BRIC (Brazil, Russia, India, and China) nations as one market.
- Megacities-specific competencies focus on large metropolitan areas. A megacity is defined as a metropolitan area with a total population in excess of ten million people. There were 23 megacities in 2011, and the number of megacities is projected to increase to 37 in 2025.[12] Examples of megacities include New York City, Mexico City, London, Moscow, Karachi, Delhi, Tokyo, and Jakarta. Another implication of a global workplace and a borderless workforce is the need to localize the learning function. A country's culture and economic ideology can influence how individuals learn and how they view the training, educational, and learning process. A single approach to training and development may not work in every region or country. As such, in certain regions and countries there can be pressure to localize the learning function to comply with local values, laws, and regulations. Corporate learning professionals must make the effort to understand local laws, practice, level of employee skills and knowledge, and employer obligations to improve the probability of achieving required learning and development objectives.

Talent Management: A Surplus of Workers and a Shortage of Required Competencies

Talent management refers to an approach that organizations use to attract, develop, retain, and mobilize employees who are most valuable and important to their strategic success, both domestically and internationally. *Attraction* entails putting policies and practices in place to recruit and select talent. Developing includes policies and practices that provide talented individuals with work and career-related competencies. *Retaining* refers to developing policies and practices that deter talent from leaving an organization. *Mobilizing* includes implementing policies and practices that facilitate movement of talent across regions and countries.

An important notion behind talent management is *talent shortage*, which occurs when employers cannot find skilled individuals in the workforce to fill positions. As Table 1.3 indicates, talent shortages are a serious concern for many organizations in a majority of countries in times of economic prosperity, as well as in times of economic uncertainty and economic/financial recession. For many organizations, especially in the service sector, shortages become severe across a wide range of positions when economic conditions improve.

Table 1.3 Top Five Countries with Talent Shortages

2011[13]	2012[14]	2013[15]
1. Japan	1. Japan	1. Japan
2. India	2. Brazil	2. Brazil
3. Brazil	3. Bulgaria	3. India
4. Australia	4. U.S.A.	4. Turkey
5. Taiwan	5. India	5. Hong Kong

Source: ManpowerGroup's research on Global Talent Shortage

There are three important reasons why employers have difficulty sourcing or finding talent:

- **There is a gap between the competencies applicants have and those that are needed to be effective:** This can occur when job requirements change rapidly or when there is a mismatch between the competencies that employers require and what the workforce can provide.

- **There are few or no available applicants:** This can happen when there is not an ample supply of talent to meet labor demands. In certain industries and occupations such as health care, demand for talent is growing at a faster pace than the availability of talent.

- **Organizations use rigorous selection procedures to screen out external candidates:** When selection criteria are too stringent or when organizations are risk-averse with respect to hiring external unknown talent, they face hiring challenges. Ultimately, the organization's focus is more on developing existing employees.

In the context of talent shortages, the challenge for the learning function is to ensure that the organization is developing current employees for future roles and positions. Providing training and development to current employees is a popular strategy used by most organizations to retain talent.

Workforce Segmentation: Various Employee Groups

Workforce segmentation refers to the process of identifying distinct groups of employees and designing human resources practices for each group based on their unique needs and characteristics. Segmentation can be done in many ways depending on an organization's business and human resources strategies.

Generational-Based Workforce Segmentation

Demographic trends in the United States are changing and will continue to do so during the next four decades. There are now five generations of employees with their own unique work-related values and attitudes toward learning and career development:

- **Traditionalists (born between 1922 and 1945)**
- **Baby boomers (born between 1946 and 1964)**
- **Generation X (born between 1965 and 1980)**
- **Generation Y or Millennial (born between 1981 and 2000)**
- **Generation Z (born after 2000)**

Table 1.4 highlights each generation's work values.[16] Attitudes toward learning are discussed in detail in Chapter 6, "Customized Learning and Learner Control."

It is estimated that the 55 years of age and older age group will total 97.8 million in 2020, which means that the group will comprise approximately 28.7% of the resident population; in 2010, this number was 24.7%.[17] This age group, referred to as baby boomers, is not retiring at traditional retirement age. Hence, they continue to work or seek work. In general, they work for a considerable length of time after reaching retirement age. For the baby boomer generation in particular, retirement age is viewed as fluid. In instances such as this, the role of the learning function is to minimize any adverse reactions to these workers by managing positive and negative biases toward them in the workplace.[18]

Table 1.4 Work-Related Values and Attitudes

Traditionalists Born between 1922 and 1945 Ages: 68–86	Experienced the Great Depression, World War II, and several societal and economic changes during their lives
	• Value job security and hard work
	• Tend to be thorough, formal, and loyal to their employers
	• Comfortable with stability; respect chain of command and institutional hierarchy
Baby boomers Born between 1946 and 1964 Ages: 49–67	Grew up during a period of relative prosperity, safety, and optimism
	• Value compensation and monetary benefits
	• Tend to embrace the social ideology of live-to-work and view work as a vehicle to financial wealth and success
	• Favor individualism and expect to be rewarded for good performance
Generation X Born between 1965 and 1980 Ages: 33–48	Grew up surrounded by financial, economic, and social insecurity
	• Have the mentality of live-to-work and not overly loyal to their employers
	• Tend to be individualistic, goal-oriented, self-reliant, unstructured, impatient, informal, and results-driven
	• Comfortable with challenging the status quo
Generation Y or Millennials Born between 1981 and 2000 Ages: 13–32	Grew up in an era of technological advances and changes
	• Motivated by jobs that provide growth, flexibility, mobility, and a sense of purpose and meaning
	• Comfortable with multitasking, change and innovation, and prefer instant and real-time feedback
	• Value social responsibility and environmental concerns
Generation Z Born after 2000	Are growing up in a world that is highly connected, interactive, uncertain, and open
	• Are curious, globally focused, impatient, and social-media savvy
	• Comfortable with big data, gamification, real-time virtual communication, and multitasking
	• Desire mobility, pursue entrepreneurial endeavors, and embrace change and abstraction

Conversely, when baby boomers do retire (and for those who have retired), the loss of knowledge and experience they take with them is cause for concern for many organizations.[19] The role of the learning function here is to facilitate the transfer of knowledge from older workers to other workers in the organization.[20]

Diversity-Based Workforce Segmentation

The U.S. workforce is becoming more diverse and will continue this pattern in the coming years. According to recent data, approximately 16% of the labor force is Hispanic, 12% is African American, and 5% is Asian.[21] It is estimated that the proportion of people of color participating in the workforce will continue to increase as the United States becomes more racially and ethnically diverse.[22] In addition, immigration is now a core source of labor supply and strongly contributes to the racial and ethnic makeup of the U.S. workforce.[23] It is estimated that 16% of the labor force is foreign-born (16 years old and over)[24] and current trends suggest that immigration will only increase, making the U.S. workforce culturally and linguistically diverse. Finally, women make up 47% of the labor force and their labor force participation has grown dramatically over the past few decades and will continue to do so.[25]

Talent-Based Workforce Segmentation[26]

Here, the focus is on categorizing employees into A, B, and C players based on the assumption that employees who add more value to the organization should be treated differently.[27] The most talented employees who have the most significant impact on the organization's business are categorized as A players (also known as high potentials). B players are talented employees who perform consistently and satisfactorily. C players are poor performers who are considered a liability; they are most likely to be separated from the organization. Using this approach, employees can also be categorized in terms of strategic/ nonstrategic and core/noncore.[28]

An important challenge for the learning function is to manage, motivate, train, and develop each group differently.

Careers: Hybrid Careers and Fluid Jobs

Organizations, careers, and jobs are changing at a rapid pace and are having a profound impact on how we work, where we work, and with whom we work. In the past, organizations were hierarchical, stable, predictable, and bureaucratic. Jobs were defined narrowly and functionally. Careers were stable and career paths were clearly defined. Most people remained on their jobs for a long time and there was job security. People mainly moved within an organization. An important assumption in terms of the employer-employee relationship was that the employer would provide stable and continued work in exchange for the employee's loyalty and good performance. Now the picture is much different. Organizations are flatter and decentralized with less hierarchy and bureaucracy. The employer-employee relationship is short term and transactional. There are fewer opportunities for career and job advancement. This has resulted in *hybrid careers* and *fluid jobs* (see Table 1.5).

Table 1.5 Characteristics of Hybrid Careers and Fluid Jobs

Hybrid Careers	Fluid Jobs
• Extremely competitive and entrepreneurial	• Work organization guided by a set of specialized tasks, projects, or skills rather than a function or jobs
• No guarantee of a career in any given field	• Job security no longer guaranteed or assumed
• Frequently changing industries, occupations, and jobs	• Real-time measurement of work performance occurs
• Declining loyalty and commitment to the employer	• Employees' work can be tied to the bottom line
• Skills and knowledge provided to employers on a temporary or contractual basis	• Work from anywhere, anytime, using videoconferencing and other mobile technologies
• Multiple career paths are common—employees can simultaneously work for multiple employers	• Increasing virtual collaboration—significant time spent working in virtual teams
• Career success means different things to different people	• Increased demand for complex cognitive skills
• People manage their own careers	• Freedom to move from one project to another
• Generating multiple sources of income is a norm	

In the context of hybrid careers and fluid jobs, there are two important challenges for the learning function. First, as the nature and structure of employment continues to change, the demand for continuous learning to prepare employees for rapid change increases. Competencies can become obsolete in a short period of time. The challenge is to continuously develop a workforce. The second challenge is the extent of development—how much development is enough? Employee mobility seems to be rising, which makes it more difficult for organizations to retain employees after development.

Learning Technologies: Continue to Evolve

Learning technologies continue to advance exponentially and have come a long way in the last few decades. Social networking, mobile learning, gaming, virtual reality, and cloud learning have improved access to content, reduced instructional time, increased the amount of content available to learners, reduced the cost of delivering training, increased collaboration between instructors and learners,[29] and increased the importance of the learning function within the organization.[30] Two interrelated themes have emerged over the last several years.

Learning Is Portable

Learners are not location-bound—they can now access content at their convenience, remotely, anywhere and anytime. They can connect with subject matter experts and collaborate with one another instantly and in real time. Further, they can access information on demand from Web-based database systems and progress at their own pace.

As jobs become more fluid, there is likely to be a gap in the competencies (that is, knowledge, skills, ability, behavior, and personality) that employees need to be effective. Therefore, learning is now an integral part of most jobs. Learning technologies allow employees to determine what is needed at any given time, as they are provided access to content and instructors at their convenience.

Learning Is Virtual

Virtual learning refers to technology that allows instructors and learners to connect with one another when they are separated by time and physical distance. Essentially, virtual learning has replaced traditional, face-to-face instructor-led learning, and technologies such as the Internet and learning portals are used to deliver content and courses to learners. Learners can use online learning communities to collaborate with other learners and subject matter experts.

Virtual learning technologies can also allow risk-free learning. Simulations and gaming provide learners a risk-free learning environment to practice and apply the learning that they have learned to real-life scenarios. These learning environments can mirror actual work environments.

Finally, virtual learning technologies allow learners to obtain real-time feedback and reinforcement. Real-time learning and performance data can be collected during and after learning activities and can be organized, stored, and retrieved by instructors when and as needed.

Overall, the technologies that have emerged during the past decade have the potential to revolutionize how organizations design, deliver, and evaluate learning activities and experiences. Selected technologies are discussed in Chapter 5, "Informal Learning."

Summary

This chapter presented the corporate learning function in the context of the rapidly changing learning landscape. It illustrated how several challenges are generating intense pressure on the corporate learning function to keep pace with a set of new norms for how organizations develop human resources. These challenges include globalization, talent management, workforce segmentation, hybrid careers and fluid jobs, and learning technologies. These challenges, among others, are changing the way people learn—and making investment in employee training and development more critical in determining the success of an organization than it has been in the past.

2

Adult Learning and Development

What's in this chapter:

- Learning perspectives and theories: how adults learn
- Work environment characteristics
- Learner characteristics
- Today's learner: fragmented learning

How adults learn has been an important area of exploration and inquiry for scholars and practitioners since the beginning of adult education. Understanding how adults learn allows learning professionals to design activities or experiences that are effective, efficient, and, most important, meet the learning needs of all employees. The classical approaches and theories that describe how adults learn still hold, but currently things are changing with the emergence of technology, the rapid flow of information, and easy access to knowledge. This chapter discusses topics that relate to adult learning in today's environment. The chapter highlights learning theories that are relevant today.

Learning Perspectives and Theories: How Adults Learn

Adult learning refers to a permanent change in specific competencies that results from experience (for example, foreign travel) and/ or an organized activity or event (for example, training).[1] Learning

19

involves three components: *learning environment* (the surrounding in which learning takes place), *learning process* (for example, how information and knowledge is processed by the learner), and *learning outcome* (results of the learning process, what is learned).

The learning environment plays an important role in learning and influences the learning process and the learning outcomes by facilitating communication between the learner and the various components of the learner's environment, which may include the physical or virtual setting in which learning takes place, the workplace, the instructor, the colleagues, and the social environment.

Learning outcomes can be defined in terms of specific competencies that include knowledge, skills, ability, attitude, and behavior. *Knowledge* is defined as facts, data, and information related to specific topics or subjects. Examples include knowledge about a foreign country or language and knowledge of how to use the Internet. *Skill* is defined as know-how or possessing the requisite knowledge to do something effectively. Examples include communication skills, collaborative skills, motor skills, analytical skills, and visual literacy skills. *Ability* refers to how good an individual is at applying specific knowledge or skills. Examples include one's ability to work with people from different cultures as well as work in virtual teams. *Attitude* refers to the opinions, beliefs, and emotions that predispose individuals to react or behave in certain ways. Examples include enthusiasm, organizational loyalty, and pessimism. Finally, *behavior* refers to observable work-related activities and actions that employees display in the workplace. Examples include bullying and showing coworkers respect.

The learning process—that is, how an individual processes the information and knowledge—can be explained from three major perspectives: cognitivism, behaviorism, and constructivism.[2] Each perspective not only provides an insight on how learning occurs, but also describes the factors in the learning environment that can affect learning.[3]

Cognitivism[4]

This perspective views individuals as information processors and focuses on the internal mental processes that occur when new information and knowledge are learned and retained. The learner uses mental processes such as perception and thinking to recognize and acquire information, which is then stored into memory and subsequently retrieved to solve problems.

An important assumption in cognitivism is that for learning to occur, newly acquired knowledge must build upon and fit well with existing or prior internal knowledge structures or schema. This process is known as *assimilation*. Prior knowledge accelerates the process of recognizing assimilating and applying new knowledge effectively.[5] In situations in which new knowledge cannot be seamlessly integrated with prior knowledge structures (for example, it is too different or complex), existing knowledge structures have to be modified to incorporate new knowledge. This is known as *accommodation*.

Workplace Implications

Cognitivism suggests that individuals learn best when learning is instructor-led or guided and instructional content is broken down into various parts and presented in a logical manner in which each part builds upon the previous part. Learners have to be provided with activities or exercises that allow them to connect new knowledge with their prior knowledge structures.[6] This perspective, however, has a few drawbacks. At times, it is not possible to separate complex concepts into parts, which may result in the learner receiving large amounts of information that may make knowledge recognition and acquisition difficult.[7] Overall, learning might not occur if the learner does not have prior knowledge structures.[8]

Behaviorism[9]

This perspective views learning as a change in immediate and observable behavior. The notion of operant conditioning is used to describe how learning occurs. *Operant conditioning* describes learning in terms of using reinforcement or punishment to modify behavior.[10] *Reinforcement* strengthens the likelihood of a particular response or behavior, and in contrast, *punishment* weakens the likelihood of a particular response or behavior.

Positive reinforcement occurs when a learner is rewarded after exhibiting desired behaviors. The learner receives something he likes. More than likely, the learner will repeat the desired behaviors. Examples of positive reinforcers include positive feedback and verbal praise. *Negative reinforcement* occurs when an unpleasant outcome is removed after a particular behavior is exhibited. The learner performs a behavior to avoid an undesirable or unpleasant outcome. Hence, by removing the unpleasant consequence, the likelihood of the particular behavior occurring again in the future increases. For example, if a learner does not participate in a leadership development program, she will not be considered for promotion. She will attend the leadership development program to be considered for promotion, hence strengthening the behavior of participating in the leadership development program.

In the context of adult learning and development that occurs in the workplace, reinforcement plays a more effective role than punishment in modifying behavior. It is more practical to reinforce desired behavior than to suppress undesirable behavior.[11]

Workplace Implications

Behaviorism, in general, suggests that instructors play a vital role in the learning process and individuals learn best in an instructor-led classroom setting where behaviors can be observed and measured clearly. Learners should be provided with clear directions as well as quick and detailed feedback after completing a learning activity. Several criticisms of this perspective, however, have been advanced.[12] Behaviorism assumes the presence of a controlled, instructor-led classroom setting. This type of setting may prevent learners from applying acquired knowledge to new and different situations in the workplace.[13] Similarly, behaviorism also ignores the cognitive process that is involved in learning.

Combination of the Behaviorism and Cognitivism Perspectives: Social Learning Theory

One of the most significant theories in the field of workplace learning and development is social learning theory,[14] which applies both the cognitivism and behaviorism perspectives to learning. This theory provides a conceptual basis for understanding how adults learn and how learning from either a training program or a developmental experience can enhance competency. This theory can also be used to design training programs and developmental experiences.

According to social learning theory, an individual's social environment is an important source of learning. Individuals learn from their practical experiences and by observing other individuals.[15] The person being observed is referred to as the *model* and the behavior being mimicked is referred to as *modeled behavior.* New information and knowledge are cognitively processed before being learned or before actually influencing behavior. In other words, cognitive change occurs first, which then leads to learning and behavioral changes.[16]

The social learning process includes four components: attention, retention, reproduction, and motivation.

Attention involves the learner observing and focusing on the model/modeled behavior and the results or consequences of the model's behavior. The assumption here is that for learning to take place, the individual has to first pay attention to new behavior. How much attention a person devotes to this exercise is dependent on several factors, including the uniqueness, credibility, and attractiveness of the model; the behaviors that need to be observed; the learner's ability to observe and pay attention; and the learner's prior experience with paying attention to observed behaviors.[17]

Retention is the process of coding the observed behavior to store it into memory as mental images or verbal descriptions. The assumption here is that the learner has to retain and remember new behavior to recall it at a later stage.

Reproduction allows the learner to duplicate or experience the modeled behavior and the consequences of exhibiting the behavior. The individual can then compare the learned behavior with what was observed (that is, modeled behavior). The learner is more likely to adapt a particular behavior if it results in a positive outcome. Several factors can facilitate the reproduction process, including how well the learner remembers the observed behavior, the learner's physical ability to reproduce the learned behavior, and the extent of feedback the learner receives with respect to how close the learned behavior is to the observed behavior.[18]

Motivation plays an important role in determining the extent to which the learner acquires, retains, and reproduces the modeled behavior. The learner can be motivated through intrinsic and extrinsic motivation to retain the new behaviors for future use. Similar to behaviorism, reinforcement (positive and negative) plays an important role in motivation. That is, behaviors that are reinforced are stored in the individual's long-term memory for likely use in the future.[19] In addition to motivation, *self-efficacy* is a crucial part of social learning theory. Self-efficacy is defined as an individual's belief in her ability to behave in a particular way to produce a desirable outcome.[20] Individuals who possess a heightened level of self-efficacy are more likely to engage in certain behaviors because they believe they can execute those behaviors successfully. In the context of social learning theory, these individuals put forth more effort and intensity to observe and learn new behaviors; subsequently, they retain and reproduce these behaviors at a later stage.

Workplace Implications

Examples of training or developmental programs based on social learning theory include cross-cultural training, expatriate training, and global leadership development experiences. These programs include instructional methods that highlight appropriate and inappropriate workplace behaviors and can include videos, role-playing, and simulations. Instructors or trainers reinforce modeled behaviors and provide relevant feedback to guide learners through the process of imitating the modeled behavior. In addition, social learning theory suggests that a successful learning experience requires extensive interaction between the instructor and the learners.

Constructivism[21]

This perspective views the learner as the main agent in creating knowledge. The learner constructs his perception of reality instead of accepting what is presented by others.[22] An individual's environment is an important source of learning. Knowledge is acquired through personal and work-related experiences; it is also acquired through interaction with others. Individuals create new knowledge and assign meaning to new knowledge through observation and reflection.[23] In essence, knowledge is highly dependent on context.[24]

An important assumption of constructivism is that learning needs to be learner-centric. Accordingly, individual characteristics play an important role in how an individual acquires knowledge. These characteristics include prior knowledge (for example, how much the learner knows about the subject), maturity (for example, prior experiences the learner had with managing and connecting different types of knowledge), and self-management skills (for example, how the learner monitors, controls, and evaluates learning).

Workplace Implications

Constructivism places the learner at the heart of learning. Learners and instructors should work together to design training or developmental programs. Understanding the learner's point of view is of critical importance to achieve a good learning environment. For example, the learner can provide her point of view with respect to developing learning goals. The role of the instructor is more of a facilitator of learning rather than a provider of knowledge. Learning activities that encourage discussion, collaboration, open-ended questions, and application of learning to real-life situations go a long way toward motivating learners to learn effectively. A major criticism of constructivism, however, is that because each person develops his understanding and interpretation of knowledge, the whole process of knowledge creation and knowledge itself becomes subjective.

The previous three perspectives, which explain how adults learn, have foundation in pedagogy. *Pedagogy* is defined as the art and science of educating and teaching children. In the pedagogical process, the learner is dependent on the teacher who makes decisions about what needs to be learned, how it should be taught, and why it needs to be taught. Learning is generally structured in such a way that the learner moves from one phase to another with guidance from her teacher. This approach can work for the majority of adult learning programs and experiences, but there are several limitations. Furthermore, adults learn differently. They have different needs from those of children and adolescents. Adults face a variety of challenges when it comes to learning, including financial, work-related, and personal difficulties. These challenges are barriers against participating in learning.

One learning theory that exclusively focuses on how adults learn is Malcolm Knowles's *andragogy* theory.[25] This theory specifically describes how adults learn and posits six important assumptions:[26]

- Adults need to know why they should learn something.
- Adults are self-directed and responsible for their own decisions.
- Adults have a rich source of prior experiences that provide an important source of learning.
- Adults are eager to learn what is necessary to cope with real-life situations.
- Adults are motivated to learn when their knowledge can solve real problems.
- Adults respond better to internal motivators (for example, self-esteem) than external motivators (for example, promotion).

Each of the learning perspectives explored provide different lenses and approaches to learning.[27] Cognitivism's main focus is on *instructional content*—how complex concepts are broken down into different parts and then processed by the human brain. In behaviorism, focus is placed on the *expert*—how the instructor provides reinforcement to encourage the repetition of correct behaviors. Conversely, in constructivism, focus is placed on the *learner*—how she constructs knowledge from past experiences and interactions.

The three perspectives can be used to design learning programs and experiences. Which perspective to use depends on the learning goals to be achieved. If the learning goals are cognitive (that is, to increase knowledge), then cognitivism may be appropriate. Behaviorism can be appropriate if learning goals are behavioral (for example, to improve performance). Learning goals that focus on helping learners explore or discover a new area can benefit from constructivism.

Work Environment Characteristics

As mentioned previously, each learning perspective provides insight into how learning occurs and what role an individual's environment and individual characteristics play in learning. The work environment is essential for learning to take place. One important factor in the individual's work environment is the organization's *learning culture,* which refers to the values, policies, and practices that encourage, engage, and motivate the individual to build upon existing competencies. There are three important characteristics of a learning culture: high-impact learning systems, learning-focused jobs, and dedicated talent management function. See Chapter 7, "Continuous Learning," for more information.

High-Performance Learning Systems (HPLS)[28]

This refers to a specific set of training and development policies and practices that work together in a system to provide learning solutions that improve individual and organizational performance. The idea behind HPLS is that they enhance or increase employees' competencies, motivation to learn, and commitment to continuous learning. Examples include

- Access to corporate university programs
- Training programs and developmental experiences based on a thorough needs assessment
- A large number of learning hours per employee
- Coaching and mentoring for employees
- Cross-training programs for employees and supervisors
- Data-driven learning evaluations
- Mobile learning platforms
- Social learning platforms
- Recognition or rewards for employees who participate in training

Learning-Focused Jobs

These jobs have extensive learning requirements and require continuous or ongoing learning so that employees may acquire new competencies. Skill requirements for these jobs are constantly changing. Employees are required to learn new skills or update existing skills to cope with impending change and to perform successfully in their current positions. For these jobs, learning activities may include working with knowledgeable coworkers or subject matter experts, learning by observing others, attending required training or developmental programs, and social learning through networking tools.

Dedicated Talent Management Function[29]

This includes a dedicated set of talent management professionals and specific policies and practices that maximize the development of high potentials or A player employees. As mentioned in Chapter 1, "Forces Shaping the Corporate Learning Function," these employees perform at a superior level and they have the ability to transition into leadership roles. Examples of talent management policies and practices include leadership development programs, stretch assignments, and individualized career development planning.

Learner Characteristics

Individual characteristics predispose people to learn, think, and behave in certain ways across a variety of situations. Although there are many individual characteristics, two relevant characteristics that can influence learning include motivation to learn and the big five personality traits.

Motivation to Learn

This refers to an individual's desire and willingness to learn.[30] Motivation to learn is a strong predictor of participation in learning activities[31] and can be influenced by a variety of factors, including how confident a person is in his own ability to learn, how committed the individual is to his job and organization, what stage the person is at as it relates to career planning, and how old the person is.[32] The design of the training or developmental program can also influence an individual's motivation to learn based on how relevant the instructional content is to the individual's job, the quality of guidance and feedback received from instructors, and the duration of the learning activity.

The Big Five Personality Traits

Personality is generally described as traits that are peculiar to a specific person and traits that predispose people to behave in certain ways, given particular situations.[33] There are several personality traits that can influence learning in adults. Among the most widely used are the "Big Five":[34]

- **Extroversion:** Being sociable, talkative, assertive, outgoing, and active
- **Agreeableness:** Being polite, good-natured, helpful, trusting, cooperative, and tolerant
- **Conscientiousness:** Being organized, careful, dependable, and goal-oriented
- **Emotional stability:** Being calm, self-confident, relaxed, and cool-minded
- **Openness to experience:** Being inquisitive, creative, imaginative, broad-minded, and philosophical

Each personality trait can affect learning differently.[35] Individuals who are extroverts are assertive and outgoing; hence, they are more likely to benefit from learning activities that require interpersonal interactions. Individuals who are high on agreeableness tend to be cooperative; they can benefit from team-based learning. Individuals who are highly conscientious are organized and dependable; they can benefit from asynchronous online learning. Individuals who are high on openness to experience are more creative and imaginative; hence, they are more likely to benefit from experiential learning. Finally, emotional stability is useful in a variety of learning environments, especially in situations that require individuals to learn from interpersonal relationships or learning activities that can include high levels of anxiety such as stretch assignments.

In addition to motivation to learn and the big five personality traits, four other individual characteristics can influence learning:

- **Cognitive ability:** This is defined as an individual's capacity to recognize, acquire, process, retain, and apply information.[36]

- **Goal orientation:** This refers to the learner's goal in the learning environment.[37] A person can have a *learning goal orientation* (focuses on developing competencies) or a *performance goal orientation* (focuses on demonstrating competence and seeking favorable evaluations).[38]

- **Locus of control:** This is defined as the individual's perception that she has influence over events and outcomes (internal locus of control) or that he or he has no control over events or outcomes (external locus of control).[39]

- **Learning styles:** This refers to the preference an individual has for acquiring and processing knowledge. Over time, people develop a preference for a particular learning style, which influences how they perceive learning. There are several types of learning styles,[40] and two popular types include sensory modality-based learning styles and learning modalities identified in Kolb's Learning Styles Inventory.

Sensory modality-based learning styles include *visual* (preference for learning by seeing or observing), *auditory* (preference for learning by hearing and sound), and *kinesthetic* (preference for learning by doing) learning styles.

Kolb's Learning Styles Inventory includes four learning styles: *diverger* (focuses on feeling and watching), *assimilator* (focuses on thinking and watching), *converger* (focuses on thinking and doing), and *accommodator* (focuses on feeling and doing). These four learning styles are based on two dimensions of learning ability.[41] The first dimension is concrete experience (feeling) versus abstract conceptualization (thinking). The second dimension is active experimentation (doing) versus reflective observation (watching).

Today's Learner: Fragmented Learning[42]

So what is different today? The forces discussed in Chapter 1 are certainly changing the landscape of adult learning. Figure 2.1 highlights the changes that have taken place in terms of the learner characteristics that are required today, the learning environment, and the learning main tools that are currently available.

As Figure 2.1 illustrates, the changes are profound, affecting every aspect of the adult learning process. Today's learner has evolved over time. He focuses more on what information is needed, customizes, learns simultaneously from multiple sources, knows how to access and filter information, and learns visually. The learning environment has also changed. Knowledge has become an integral part of lives; continuous learning is required to prevent skill obsolescence; there is a blurring of boundaries between work and learning; and learners are expected to have control over their learning and be self-directed.

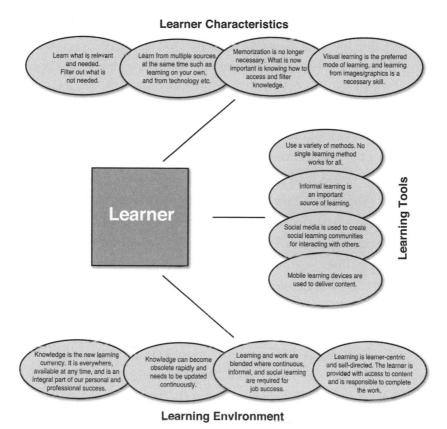

Figure 2.1 Required learning characteristics, learning environment, and available learning tools

Finally, the tools for learning have significantly changed. There's no one learning tool that is appropriate for everybody; informal learning is becoming increasingly important; social learning is now a key learning tool; and mobile learning has transformed how content is delivered to learners.

In the context of the changes taking place, an important question is whether the classical theories of adult learning are relevant today. The answer depends on who you ask. Behaviorism, cognitivism, and constructivism can still describe the learning process of the contemporary learner but what has changed now is that the three perspectives interact and depend on each other to describe the process of learning. The three perspectives are not distinct. The learning process today is a combination of cognitivism, behaviorism, and constructivism and can be described as fragmented or piecemeal learning.

Fragmented learning involves noticing and acquiring knowledge in bits and pieces, as information comes along through a variety of sources, such as attending a workshop, observing correct behaviors, completing an online tutorial, browsing the Internet, reading books, and interacting with colleagues. This process of acquiring knowledge or observing behaviors can be explained by cognitivism and behaviorism. Next, the individual switches from one concept to another depending on what is important and relevant to the individual rather than follow a predefined structure or process. This process of choosing what to focus on is similar to creating or designing knowledge and can be explained by constructivism. Then, at some point, like a jigsaw puzzle, the individual figures out how the concepts are interrelated and puts the different parts together, connecting one concept with the other to produce the final knowledge structure. This is referred to as aggregation of knowledge.

Successful aggregation of knowledge rests on the assumption that individuals understand the rules for connecting different concepts and are aware of the conditions under which these connections can take place. An *inductive approach to learning* is useful here.[43] This approach suggests that the individual learns a specific topic by exploring and observing specific examples that eventually lead to more general conclusion or concepts; that is, the learner goes from the specific to the general. The role of the instructor in inductive learning is that of a facilitator who designs an environment that allows the learner to explore new topics or concepts, notice patterns or trends among those concepts, and solve problems.

In addition to inductive learning, activities that integrate new concepts into the learner's prior knowledge (for example, what she already knows) are necessary for successful aggregation of knowledge. Without relevant prior knowledge structures or experience, the learner is vulnerable to illogical conclusions. Prior knowledge allows the learner to assimilate new knowledge into memory and build on what the learner already knows.[44] Learning occurs when the new knowledge is related to prior accumulated knowledge.

Overall, fragmented learning is a result of the changes taking place within the learning industry (refer to Figure 2.1). It is important to note, however, that organizations have to satisfy the learning needs of a variety of employee groups, each with its own distinct concerns and motivations and each requiring an entirely different approach to learning. In other words, fragmented learning may explain how a particular group learns; there are still employee groups that may learn in the traditional manner.

Summary

This chapter focused on how adults learn and develop. Specifically, it provided definitions, terminology, and insight into how adults learn and develop as individuals. The chapter described three major perspectives on how individuals process information and knowledge:

cognitivism, behaviorism, and constructivism. Next, the chapter provided an insight on how a specific factor in the individual's work environment can affect learning. Then the chapter discussed how individual characteristics such as motivation to learn and the big five personality traits predispose people to learn, think, and behave in certain ways across a variety of situations. Finally, the chapter closed with a discussion of fragmented learning.

3

The Art of Knowledge Acquisition

What's in this chapter:

- Knowledge economy and the knowledge workforce
- Different types and levels of knowledge
- Knowledge search
- Information overload
- Knowledge transfer

Organizations today are increasingly dependent on *knowledge-based resources* for creating growth, wealth, and profits.[1] Knowledge-based resources can exist at different levels. At the *individual level*, knowledge-based resources include the knowledge possessed by employees (what each employee knows). At the *group level*, knowledge-based resources include the collective knowledge of the group members (what the team knows). At the *organizational level*, knowledge-based resources include the collective knowledge of various parts of the organization (what different functions such as HR or marketing know). Finally, at the *technological level*, knowledge-based resources include the various types of knowledge that might be present in different technologies, such as computers, tablets, smartphones, electronic databases, Internet, intranet, cloud-based systems, and social media platforms. Regardless of the level, knowledge-based resources can provide organizations with sustainable competitive advantage when the knowledge-based resources are difficult to articulate and imitate.[2]

Managing knowledge effectively is critical to the performance and competitiveness of an organization, especially in service-based industries such as health care, finance, banking, research and development, and management consulting. The knowledge management process includes *acquisition* (obtaining knowledge), *storage* (keeping knowledge), *maintenance* (updating knowledge), *retrieval* (using knowledge), and *transfer* (moving knowledge). An important component in this process is knowledge acquisition, which is critical. Knowledge has to be created first, and the quality of the acquired knowledge provides the foundation for the rest of the components, beginning with acquisition and working up to transfer.

The knowledge needs of today's learners are changing. They are required to acquire knowledge quickly and accurately in any given environment. They have to learn rapidly and have to learn correctly to remain competitive—knowledge-seeking skills are as important as learning. This chapter focuses on issues related to knowledge acquisition at the individual level.

Knowledge Economy and the Knowledge Workforce

If there is one factor that is the most important determinant of how individuals acquire knowledge, it is the existence of a *knowledge economy*.[3] There are various definitions of a knowledge economy, but an overall theme that cuts across most definitions is that in a knowledge economy, *knowledge* is an essential factor of production that is equal, if not superior, to other types of factors of production (for example, natural, physical, and financial).[4] From an organization's perspective, there are certain core characteristics of a knowledge economy:[5]

- There is an *abundance of knowledge-intensive industries*, such as pharmaceutical, education, scientific research and development, management consulting, accounting services, banking and financial services, legal services, and health-care services. These industries include *knowledge-intensive firms* that depend on knowledge-based resources to produce goods and services.

- Organizations *use extensive technology-based resources* to connect with workers, customers, partner organizations, and other key stakeholders in real time (for example, Internet-based companies).[6]

- Organizations *depend on the knowledge that is created by others*[7] (for example, customers and competitors) and on the *flow of knowledge* that occurs between/among individuals, groups, and organizations (for example, between a company and its supplier).

- Organizations *form alliances or partnerships with other firms to gain knowledge* and *learn from each other*.[8] In recent years, there has been an emergence of joint ventures. (For example, a new business entity, the joint venture, is created by two or more partner firms.) Joint ventures are largely used to gain knowledge from partners to transfer that knowledge back to parent firms.[9]

- *Continuous learning is essential for all employees in the organization*. Learning is ongoing and a continuous process that helps employees and eventually the organization to adapt to changes in its environment.

A knowledge economy requires a *knowledge workforce,* which refers to employees known as *knowledge workers*.[10] The traditional perspective of knowledge workers describes these individuals as having advanced professional or technical qualifications and extensive work experience (for example, doctors, lawyers, scientists, and programmers). This may still hold true, but in today's knowledge economy, the definition of a knowledge worker is more inclusive of different types of workers. Characteristics of a knowledge workforce include workers who

- Compete with each other on the basis of how current and updated their knowledge is.
- Quickly locate relevant information, assess the quality or the usefulness of the information, and filter or discard what is not needed.
- Continuously update and maintain their human capital by taking professional development courses, seminars, and workshops.
- Stay current with the latest business and industry trends.
- Add value to the organization by applying what they know and what they learn.
- Constantly search for new or better career opportunities—the job search never stops.
- Always seek to increase their social capital by interacting with people through social media platforms, virtual communities, mentoring, and voluntarism.

These knowledge economy and knowledge workforce characteristics create unique changes for the learning function, such as transferring knowledge from one location/person to another. In addition, the learning function has to play an important role in how an organization develops knowledge workers, in particular contingent or part-time knowledge workers who take with them important human capital when they leave.[11]

The Different Types and Levels of Knowledge

There are many possible ways to describe knowledge. It is important to understand that all types of knowledge are not the same; certain types of knowledge are more valuable to the organization than others. Knowledge can be described in terms of type and quality. *Type* refers to characteristics of the knowledge. Table 3.1 describes the different types of knowledge, each with its own unique characteristics. *Quality* refers to how useful the knowledge is. Table 3.2 describes the different qualities of knowledge.

Table 3.1 Different Types of Knowledge

Knowledge Type	Description
Tacit versus explicit	*What type of knowledge is easily coded and articulated?*
	Explicit knowledge can be coded, easily communicated with others, and stored (for example, a memo). Tacit knowledge is not visible, is difficult to articulate, is difficult to define, and is not easily shared with others. It is context-specific and generally acquired through experience (for example, cultural beliefs and values).
Generic versus specific	*What type of knowledge is applied to a variety of situations and contexts?*
	Generic knowledge has wide applicability and can be applied to a variety of situations, business units, and organizations (for example, a procedure for design training programs). Specific knowledge focuses on a specific topic and can be applied to particular areas within an organization (for example, functional knowledge such as marketing knowledge, HR knowledge, and accounting knowledge).
Declarative versus procedural	*What type of knowledge involves knowing how to do something?*
	Declarative knowledge includes factual information and focuses on the question of "what." (For example, "what is the sales tax rate in New York?") Procedural knowledge focuses on the question of "how," that is, how to do something. (For example, "How do you evaluate an online training program?")

Knowledge Type	Description
Sticky versus movable	*What type of knowledge is difficult to move from one location/environment/person to another?*
	Sticky knowledge[12] is not easily transferable within the organization. It is difficult or slow to move from one *location/environment/person* to another because it works well for one group (for example, a developmental program for high potentials). Movable knowledge is easily transferable across the organization (for example, training best practices).

Table 3.2 Different Levels or Quality of Knowledge

Knowledge Level	Description
Superficial versus deep	*What type of knowledge is comprehensive and in-depth?*
	Superficial knowledge is incomplete and vague. It lacks thoroughness, substance, and significance. Deep knowledge is clear, comprehensive, well structured, and thorough in terms of its coverage. (For example, experts have deep knowledge.)
Fragmented versus whole	*What type of knowledge reflects a complete concept?*
	Fragmented knowledge reflects part of a concept rather than the whole concept. It is difficult to connect to the broader concept or phenomenon. Whole knowledge reflects a complete concept or phenomenon. It is an integration of the various parts that go into forming a concept.

Tacitness, Specificity, and Competitive Advantage

As mentioned earlier, not all types of knowledge are equivalent. Certain types of knowledge are more useful than others. From an organization's point of view, two knowledge characteristics are critical with respect to creating competitive advantage: *extent of tacitness* (tacit versus explicit) and *extent of specificity* (specific versus generic). From what we know, tacit knowledge is considered more valuable to organizations than explicit knowledge. Tacit knowledge is difficult to codify and, hence, imitate or copy (conditions necessary for having a competitive advantage). Similarly, knowledge that is highly specific is not easily transferable; it is not mobile and, hence, is more valuable to the organization (than generic knowledge).

Figure 3.1 illustrates the interplay between tacitness and specificity in terms of which combination of tacitness and specificity is most useful to the organization. The horizontal axis displays the extent of specificity (generic knowledge versus specific knowledge) and the vertical axis shows the extent of tacitness (tacit knowledge versus explicit knowledge). The first quadrant includes knowledge that is tacit and generic. The second quadrant has knowledge that is explicit and generic. This is the least valuable combination because it is easy to codify and copy. The third quadrant consists of knowledge that is specific and explicit. The fourth quadrant consists of knowledge that is specific and tacit. This combination is the most useful because this type of knowledge is difficult to articulate and copy by others.

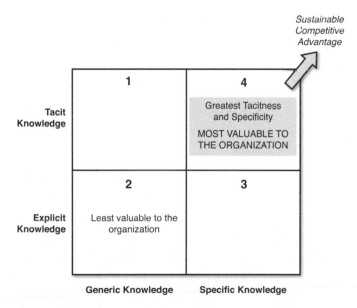

Figure 3.1 Interplay between tacitness and specificity

Knowledge Search

How people search for knowledge has become a popular topic in human resources management for a number of sound reasons. First, the notion of acquiring knowledge and its consequences extends beyond the obvious workplace—as mentioned in the previous chapter, knowledge has become an integral part of our lives. We seek knowledge all the time. Our knowledge-seeking behaviors at home impact our knowledge-seeking behaviors at work and vice versa. Second, our employers, our colleagues, and our friends and family all assume that we know *how* to search for information and *how* to acquire the knowledge we need. Finally, the quality of information and knowledge we acquire has significant impact on our work life and career development.

Approaches to Knowledge Acquisition

Currently, there are several traditional perspectives on how people acquire knowledge, along with a growing number of criticisms. A few of the perspectives are rooted in philosophical traditions. This section briefly highlights four traditional perspectives on how knowledge is acquired.

The first perspective is *intuition*, which suggests that knowledge is acquired on the basis of personal instincts or feelings that could be accurate or inaccurate, causing the quality of knowledge to be poor some of the time. The second perspective is *authoritarian*, which proposes that knowledge is acquired from an expert who is well versed in the relevant domain or topic. The expert can be a person (for example, a trainer) or an electronic device (for example, a computer-based program or video). The third perspective is *rationalism*, which suggests that knowledge is derived from reasons and proofs. Finally, the fourth perspective, *empiricism*, points out that knowledge is acquired through experience, scientific experimentation, and observation.

So how do people search for knowledge today? One possibility is to integrate these perspectives to fully explain the phenomenon of knowledge acquisition in the digital age. In other words, how people acquire knowledge can be visualized as a multiperspective phenomenon, a combination of intuition, authoritarian, rationalism, and empiricism. Regardless of the approach people use to acquire knowledge, an important question is: What methods do people use to search for information? (Remember, information leads to knowledge.) There are a variety of methods, such as the Internet, mobile smartphones or tablets, electronic books, digital libraries, traditional books, social media, physical libraries, professional journals or periodicals, encyclopedias, newspapers, and so forth. However, the majority of people today search for information by using online or Internet-based platforms.

Information Overload

According to a recent study,[13]

"In 2008, Americans consumed about 1.3 trillion hours of information outside of work, an average of almost 12 hours per person per day. Media consumption totaled 3.6 zettabytes and 1,080 trillion words, corresponding to 100,500 words and 34 gigabytes for the average person on an average day." (p.980)

This trend continues to hold and grow.

Information can be good but the problem is that it's everywhere— we are surrounded by information at work, at home, and in society at large.[14] If not managed properly, it can lead to *information overload,* which refers to having more information than you can acquire, process, store, or retrieve,[15] and it can lead to a variety of problems, such as anxiety, stress, inefficiency, and, ultimately, poor performance.

Information overload is a serious problem for everyone in the modern workplace, but more important, for the knowledge worker who has to search for information on a regular and continuous basis.

Causes of Information Overload

It is important to note that information overload means different things to different people, but there are recognized causes of information overload:[16]

- **Job/work structure:** Jobs that require extensive communication and coordination with other members of the organization can lead to greater loads.
- **Job/work complexity:** Jobs that have complex, nonroutine tasks tend to have greater information-processing requirements and, thus, can increase the information load.
- **Perceived information need:** Individuals who perceive a high information need (for example, someone who just started a new job) may acquire more information than necessary, which can eventually lead to information overload.
- **Type of information:** Information that is ambiguous, fragmented, superficial, duplicate, or poor in quality can force the individual to further research (for example, search for more information) and spend more time processing the information. This can lead to information overload.

For most people today, how we live and work can lead to information overload:

- Too much e-mail and incoming messages.
- Accumulation of old files and information over time.
- Easy access to the Internet.
- Being online most of the time.

- Constantly texting or surfing on mobile devices.

- Speed is important; information is needed quickly in real time.

- Information needs must be fulfilled immediately.

Overall, information overload is becoming a problem in all aspects of managing human resources and affecting a large number of people. Chapter 6, "Customized Learning and Learner Control," discusses how to manage information overload from a learning perspective.

Knowledge Transfer

Knowledge transfer is a process that involves the movement, transfer, sharing, or exchange of knowledge between a source and a recipient. For example, knowledge transfer can be between two individuals, between an individual and a group, between two groups, or among group members.

The success of a knowledge transfer depends on several factors, including the type of knowledge transferred and the mechanism used to transfer the knowledge. Interpersonal interaction is one type of mechanism you can to transfer knowledge; through interpersonal interactions, you can transfer knowledge from a source to a recipient.[17]

Training and development activities that use interpersonal interactions are knowledge transfer mechanisms. These activities can be categorized as high, moderate, and low intensity of transfer.[18] *High-intensity knowledge transfer mechanisms* are those that can transfer a large amount of knowledge quickly and include group-based approaches that allow greater frequency of communication, such as working in large teams.[19] High-intensity knowledge transfer mechanisms can be used to transfer tacit knowledge. *Moderate-intensity knowledge transfer mechanisms* include individuals as well as small-size groups to transfer knowledge. Activities such as coaching, mentoring, simulations, behavior modeling, or action learning work well here. Finally, *low-intensity knowledge transfer mechanisms* include didactic approaches, such as lectures and presentations.

To provide an overall example, refer to Figure 3.1. Knowledge that is highly tacit and highly specific (see the fourth quadrant) can be transferred using high-intensity knowledge transfer mechanisms. You can use low-intensity transfer mechanisms to transfer knowledge that is explicit and generic knowledge (see the second quadrant). You can use medium-intensity transfer mechanisms to transfer the different combinations of tacitness and specificity that are between the high and low end of their respective continua.[20]

Implications for the Learning Function

Based on the concepts discussed in this chapter, it seems that it is all about training and developing a knowledge workforce. For each individual employed in a knowledge economy, knowledge acquisition is a necessity. It is a means to an end; it is a step toward career development and career security. As a result, today's learner is saturated with information and knowledge. There are several implications for the learning function:

- Knowledge acquisition for the knowledge worker has to be tied to career-based incentives. That is, it has to lead to career development and growth.
- Unlearning becomes part of learning. Today's knowledge worker has to make room for new knowledge.
- Individuals can acquire several different types of knowledge and use different ways to acquire it.
- Training and development activities become tools to transfer knowledge.

The title of this chapter suggests that knowledge acquisition is an art. Similar to artwork, all learners are unique because of their unique approach to acquiring knowledge and require a unique mix of knowledge types. The right knowledge for one individual will be the wrong type for another—that's why the process of knowledge acquisition must be customized to meet the needs of each learner. This theme carries throughout the book.

Summary

This chapter focused on the various ways adults acquire knowledge and why the art of knowledge acquisition is as important as learning. The chapter started with a discussion on the knowledge economy and the knowledge worker. The chapter then described different types and levels of knowledge, such as tacit, generic, declarative, and sticky. Next, the chapter described how people search for knowledge and emphasized that the quality of information and knowledge an individual acquires has significant implications for career development. The chapter also described the important notion of information overload and how overload is a serious problem for everyone in the modern workplace. Finally, the chapter discussed the process of knowledge transfer.

Part II

Emerging Trends in Training
and Development Practices

4

Technology-Based Learning (Trend 1)

What's in this chapter:

- What is technology-based learning?
- Impact of technology on learning
- Mobile learning

A search of popular and practitioner press on the topic of *technology-based learning* or *e-learning* (both are used interchangeably) using a popular search engine resulted in more than 130,000 and 15,000,000 hits, respectively. Similarly, there is a plethora of academic research that exists on the topic. The number of consulting firms and research-based organizations examining topics related to technology and learning is also growing rapidly. If this is any indication of the popularity of the topic globally, it demonstrates that technology has had a tremendous impact on learning. Although this might be true, it is clear that learning technologies are well established and most likely will continue to evolve.

This chapter discusses the first trend: technology-based learning.

What Is Technology-Based Learning?

Technology-based learning (TBL) makes reference to technology operating as an *enabler* while also referring to learning occurring through the use of technology. Examples include the use of computers and the Internet as educational tools. Hence, technology enables learners to connect with instructional content, instructors, and other learners.

A *Historical Perspective*

The impact of technology on learning and workplace training and development can be traced back to 1970 with the emergence of computer-assisted learning (CAL) using mainframe computers.[1] It was not until the early 1980s that computers were used as instructional aids and tools in educational and workplace settings.[2] Desktop personal computers (PCs) made it possible to store, transfer, and share learning content using floppy disks. In the early 1980s, learning was one-directional and passive from the instructor to the learner with the use of the PC. With the emergence of high-resolution computer graphics and CD-ROMs in the late 1980s, learning content and activities became interactive and interesting.

The 1990s saw a significant technological impact on learning with the emergence of the Internet and later the World Wide Web (WWW),[3] which enabled new kinds of learning applications and forms of communication and collaborations. Terms or phrases such as *electronic learning* or *e-learning* became widely used in work settings, homes, and educational institutions. The availability of notebook computers introduced the portability of learning. By the late 1990s and early 2000s, important learning technologies had emerged, such as synchronous chat rooms, asynchronous discussion boards, and learning management systems. The array of technology allowed learners to access learning content when and where they chose and to engage interactively with one another. Instructors or trainers were able to share their knowledge with learners and with other instructors.

The early 2000s saw the development of high-level graphics, video, and sound that allowed media-rich content to be delivered quickly. Between 2000 and 2005, the arrival of PC tablets allowed learners to record and store notes efficiently and effectively. By 2005, mobile learning (m-learning) became popular, and by 2010,[4] the development of a variety of smart mobile devices changed the way instructors and learners communicated with one other as well as changed how they accessed learning resources. Since then, mobile learning, coupled with other emerging technologies such as social media, has provided instructors and learners with flexibility while on the move. Learners can access instructional content from anywhere, at any time.

Emerging Themes

Technology-based learning has come a long way since the 1970s. There have been great innovations in the last few years, but the area is still evolving. It is likely that we will see major improvements and developments in the near future. Moreover, some of the important technology-based learning themes that have manifested over the last few years include

- **Impact on design:** Technology has had the greatest impact on how instructional content is delivered.
- **Hybrid approaches to learning:** A blended or hybrid approach to learning is becoming popular. This approach combines traditional (in-class) face-to-face approaches with online delivery of content.
- **Continued upward investment trends:**[5] Investment in technology-based learning is increasing, particularly in technologies that use videos, games, and simulations.
- **Large organizations:**[6] Technology-based learning is more prevalent in large companies.
- **Portable learning:** There is considerable interest in using smart mobile devices to connect learners with instructional content.
- **Required training:**[7] Technology-based learning is mostly used to provide training that is required or mandatory.

- **Traditional face-to-face learning:** Instructor-led training or development, especially by instructors who are exceptional, is a premium product and difficult to replace with technology.

In addition to these themes, there are several advantages of technology-based learning.

From the organization's perspective:

- *Time to delivery* and *costs of delivery* are reduced.
- Instructors can *reach a wide variety of learners* in different locations.
- There is flexibility in *customizing instructional content* to suit each learner in terms of timing, learning needs, and learning styles.

From the learner's perspective:

- *Instructional content can be accessed* at any time, from any place in real time.
- *Simultaneous engagement and interaction with peers and the instructor* add another level of expediency to the learning process.
- *Feedback* from instructors on progress and performance is provided almost instantaneously.

Impact of Technology on Learning

The impact of technology on workplace learning can be examined using the framework shown in Figure 4.1. Based on the figure, it is clear that learners; the design and impact of learning programs, experiences, and activities; and organizational culture are greatly affected by technology. It is important to point out that technology has had the greatest impact on design or on how instructional programs, experiences, or activities are designed and delivered.

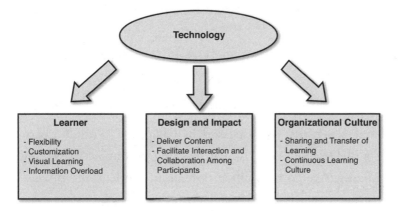

Figure 4.1 How technology impacts learning

Learner

Technology impacts individuals (learners) in a variety of ways. Four obvious ways include flexibility, customization, visual learning, and information overload.

- **Flexibility:** There is greater flexibility in accessing content from any place at any time; thus, there is more control over the learning process.

- **Customization:** As discussed in Chapter 6, "Customized Learning and Learner Control (Trend 3)," technology-based learning is not for everyone. Some individuals prefer traditional, face-to-face, instructor-led sessions and find online learning unappealing. Conversely, others prefer the opportunities and benefits that online learning brings.

  Individuals who prefer technology-based learning tend to have certain characteristics:

  - They are self-starters.
  - They can work and learn independently.

- They have good time-management skills.

- They have good written and verbal communication skills.

- They are comfortable using e-mail and online discussion boards.

- They can effectively multitask and successfully manage multiple devices and applications.

- They enjoy engaging and interacting with others virtually.

- **Visual learning:** As discussed in Chapter 2, "Adult Learning and Development," visual learning continues to become increasingly important, albeit critical, in the learning process. Everyone needs to be a visual learner.

- **Information overload:** As discussed in Chapter 3, "The Art of Knowledge Acquisition," information overload can serve as a barrier to learning for many people. Technology-based learning can lead to information overload and even technology overload.

Design and Impact

According to recent data, nearly one-third of all training content is now delivered electronically.[8] There are a variety of technologies that are used to deliver content to learners. A few can deliver content, whereas others can deliver content and facilitate interaction and collaboration among participants (learners and instructors).

The *World Wide Web* (WWW/Web) started the technology-based learning revolution. A network of interlinked hypertext documents, the Web is widely used to share information on the Internet. The Web started with Web 1.0, which was one-directional; the user passively received or accessed information. We are now using Web 2.0, which is bidirectional and allows the user to engage and interact with information, content, and other users. Web 3.0[9] is presently in the development stage and is predicted to provide greater speed, smarter searches, and improved quality of information.

Web conferencing is another technology used to share information. Content is delivered through the World Wide Web to participants who are in different locations. Web conferencing can include *webinars* or *webcasts* that allow a presenter to share content, such as presentations or videos, with participants or attendees in real time.

Other technologies that facilitate collaboration among participants include *bulletin boards* and discussion groups, which allow participants (learners and instructors) to interact through threaded discussions in a communal online space.[10] *Blogs* (similar to an online journal) are also used to share information and to promote or increase awareness of a particular topic.

Massive Open Online Courses (MOOCs), which refer to educational courses or programs that are often offered for free via the Internet, are currently used at the university or college level. Whether MOOCs can be adapted by noneducational institutions is not clear at this time. One possibility is to use MOOCs as complementary, Internet-based resources alongside other technologies such as Web conferencing.

Three technologies that are extensively used not only to deliver content, but also to facilitate learning are *simulations, games,* and *virtual worlds.* These three technologies are labeled *synthetic learning environments;* they provide a mock learning environment that replicates an actual work environment.[11]

A *simulation* allows learners to immerse themselves in a situation as if it were actually happening. Learners can explore and experience various scenarios. They can make mistakes and learn from them in real time.

Business gaming (also known as gamification) refers to using gaming concepts, such as competition and entertainment, in work-related activities.[12] Gaming metaphors are used in business activities to engage and motivate employees.[13] For example, employees can be asked to generate new ideas, and those ideas can be open to the public or consumers to view and select their favorites.[14]

A *virtual world* is an online community that allows a large number of individuals from different locations to interact with one another in simulated environments using graphical models called *avatars,* which are animated graphic images controlled by the user. Learners can practice specific tasks that can be difficult to practice at actual work or engage in a variety of learning activities.

Synthetic learning environments are important because they can provide learning when it is practically impossible, costly, or extremely dangerous to learn and practice in the actual workplace.[15]

Certain technologies are used to manage the learning process, such as Learning Management Systems (LMS). These systems have been around for a decade. They are Internet-based products or software applications that allow organizations to manage, develop, monitor, and assess learning programs or activities. Learning Management Systems are evolving as new technologies emerge and becoming more industry specific (for example, educational, banking, and health care).

Some technologies are used for the purpose of storage and retrieval of information, such as *cloud computing,* which includes software, applications, and services delivered over the Internet. Information and data are stored in the cloud and are available to users anywhere, anytime by connecting to the cloud via a computer, tablet, smartphone, or other device. Cloud computing can allow learners to access instructional content from anywhere by connecting to the cloud.

Social learning is also becoming popular with the emergence of social networks, such as Twitter, Facebook, and LinkedIn. This type of learning is dependent on interactions that take place virtually or in person, and the quality of learning is highly dependent on the quality of interactions. Whether social learning replaces any of the traditional learning methods is yet to be seen, but one thing is certain: Social learning is more aligned with informal learning, which is discussed in the next chapter.

With many learning technologies available, each with its own strengths and weaknesses, it is often challenging to select the most appropriate technology to deliver instructional content. One approach is to use a *blended* or *hybrid strategy* to deliver instructional content to learners. This approach has been around for many years and began with an integration of traditional, face-to-face instruction with technology-based learning activities.[16] In online programs, a blended strategy is often used to combine synchronous and asynchronous learning (see Chapter 9, "Extreme Development: Stretch Assignments and Learning Agility (Trend 6)," for a definition of synchronous versus asynchronous learning). Moving forward, a blended strategy will play a significant role in learning, as organizations focus on reducing costs, increasing mobility of learning, and maximizing learning.[17]

Organizational Culture

The role of technology at the organizational level has primarily been to transfer learning and share knowledge among different units of the organization. As discussed in Chapter 3, certain technologies become tools to transfer and share knowledge. For example, several of the technologies that are used to deliver content to learners can also be used to transfer learning from one individual to another. Further, other types of technologies allow for the creation of a continuous learning culture (see Chapter 7, "Continuous Learning (Trend 4)").

Mobile Learning

Recent data shows that there are more than 6 billion mobile-cellular subscriptions in the world[18] and it is estimated that more than 100 million people in the United States will have tablets and more than 200 million people will have smartphones by 2016.[19] At least over the next several years, these trends are likely to continue as more mobile technologies emerge and become available to individuals and organizations. It is clear that mobile devices are changing the way we communicate with others and how we access and manage information.

Mobile devices are portable devices that are not connected to a specific location.[20] Mobile learning is defined as using mobile devices for learning purposes. Examples include accessing instructional content, interacting with other learners and instructors, connecting to larger learning systems, such as universities or training centers, and completing learning activities.

There are several mobile devices with varying degrees of mobility that can be used in mobile learning. Figure 4.2 illustrates the major mobile technologies or devices available today in terms of their mobility. These devices can also be organized according to the extent of interaction between the user and the device. Laptop computers, tablet computers, and portable game consoles can be highly interactive. Smartphones, wearable computer glasses, and smart watches can be less interactive. E-book readers are mostly used to download content. In addition, each device provides different types of media quality output.[21]

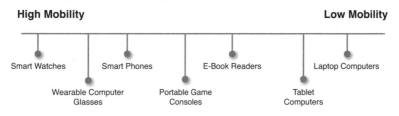

Figure 4.2 Different mobile technologies

It is important not to treat the technologies in generic terms—each technology has its own unique characteristics, including strength, weakness, design, and style. Every learning environment is unique, and the choice of mobile technology must be based on the specific needs of the learners.

Major Themes in Mobile Learning

Mobile technologies are evolving rapidly in terms of power, design, functionality, and quality. What is true today might not be true a year from now. There are, however, certain themes that have appeared as more organizations and people use mobile technologies to access, store, and manage information:

- **Alignment is important:** Mobile learning technologies have to be aligned with other technologies to provide a complete learning experience. Mobile technology can be aligned or integrated with social networking or with cloud computing.[22] For example, tablet or smartphone applications and programs can be stored in the cloud and accessed anytime and anywhere when needed.

- **Mobile learning complements other forms of learning:** Mobile learning is not a stand-alone learning technology. Most of the time, mobile learning is part of a blended learning approach; that is, it is part of a larger learning experience.[23] It is used to deliver specific, customized content to users.

- **Mobile learning facilitates on-demand learning or just-in-time learning:** Mobile learning can provide the right content to the right people at any time, regardless of location. Some learners can access content when they need it at their convenience; some can use a GPS-enabled mobile device and let the learning system find them in real time.[24]

- **Security of information and privacy is a significant concern:**[25] An organization's approach to mobile learning is guided by security and privacy concerns. Certain industries like finance, accounting, and health care are heavily regulated and have many rigorous guidelines for managing information. Firms in these industries are limited in their use of mobile technologies. This is one reason why organizations are slow in adopting mobile learning.[26]

- **Moving from Bring Your Own Devices (BYOD) to Bring Your Own Learning (BYOL):** BYOD is becoming common in the workplace. BYOD is an approach that allows employees to use their mobile devices at work. A step above BYOD is BYOL. As discussed in Chapter 5, "Informal Learning (Trend 2)," informal learning is becoming an increasingly important part of workplace learning. Many employers prefer employees to learn on their own, in their own time, and transfer that learning to work.

Overall, mobile learning fits extremely well with other trends discussed in this book, such as informal learning (Chapter 5), learner control and person-centered learning (Chapter 6), and continuous learning (Chapter 7). In other words, mobile learning technologies allow learners to learn on their own outside work, exercise control over their learning, learn what is needed and when it is needed, and continuously update their competencies.

Designing Mobile Learning

The success of a mobile learning initiative is in its design. There are certain best practices that have proven to be essential elements of any mobile learning design:

- Learning sessions or activities have to be short in duration (10–20 minutes). Some individuals have a shorter attention span when using mobile devices; others can experience fatigue when using mobile devices for a long period of time. Longer learning sessions can be broken down and distributed over time.

- Instructional content needs to be focused and targeted. Irrelevant and unnecessary topics can distract learners from what is important.

- Instructional content needs to be simple, concise, easy to follow, and easy to understand. In addition, content should be easy to maintain and update. Extreme use of graphics should be avoided.

- Selection of the mobile technology has to be done carefully. As mentioned earlier and referred to in Figure 4.2, each device is unique in terms of its characteristics. Factors that need to be considered include the level of mobility, extent of interactivity, and level of media quality.[27]

Summary

This chapter focused on technology-based learning. It began with a historical perspective, followed by a description of important technology-based learning themes that have developed over the last few years. It then explained how technology has impacted the learner, the design and impact of learning programs, and organizational culture. The chapter also discussed mobile learning in detail by explaining that each mobile technology is unique with its own strength and weakness. More important, the choice of mobile technology must support the specific needs of the learners. Overall, mobile learning has the potential to transform how organizations and individuals approach learning.

5

Informal Learning (Trend 2)

What's in this chapter:

- Different types of informal learning
- Informal learning strategy
- Who is most likely to participate in informal learning?

The concept of Bring Your Own Learning (BYOL) discussed in the previous chapter is developed around the notion that learning often occurs outside of the classroom or outside of a formal learning environment. This is not surprising. As discussed in the first chapter, jobs today require a person to be in constant learning mode, especially in this era when knowledge has an expiration date. However, it is not always practical or possible to attend formalized learning sessions. In today's world of work, there exists an invisible *learning contract* between employers and employees: Workers are expected to learn on their own to complement formalized learning that occurs at work.

The popular learning framework, "70/20/10,"[1] reflects this trend: 70% of learning occurs informally through on-the-job experiences, 20% of learning occurs through social interactions, and 10% of learning occurs via formalized sessions. More recent findings show similar trends,[2] and sometimes, based on my observations, it seems that the learning framework has now evolved into "80/10/10" or "90/5/5." Regardless of how much learning occurs on the job or outside of work, the reality is that with the emergence of social media and the development of a plethora of mobile technologies (see Chapter 4, "Technology-Based Learning (Trend 1)"), organizations recognize the potential of informal learning supporting formal learning.[3]

This chapter discusses the second trend of informal learning.

Different Types of Informal Learning

The idea of informal learning goes back several decades,[4] and since then, there have been a variety of definitions and several interpretations of informal learning.[5] Regardless of which definition is used, there is a common theme across them:

- Informal learning is experiential.
- Informal learning is learner-guided or self-directed.
- Informal learning occurs outside of a formalized or structured learning environment.

There are four types of informal learning based on two complex dimensions: *purpose* and *location.*

Purpose and location form the framework shown in Figure 5.1 that can be used to describe types of informal learning. The horizontal axis shows purpose, which refers to the willingness and motivation an individual has toward participating in informal learning. Purpose can be intentional (there is a willingness to learn and motivation) or incidental[6] (is unintentional and occurs randomly). The vertical axis shows location, which refers to where learning takes place: onsite (at work) or offsite (outside of work).

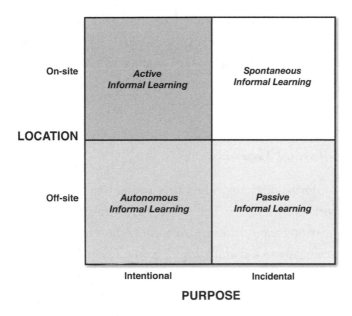

Figure 5.1 Types of informal learning

These two dimensions (purpose and location) can be used to categorize informal learning into four types:

- Active informal learning
- Autonomous informal learning
- Spontaneous informal learning
- Passive informal learning

A brief overview of these types of informal learning follows.

Active Informal Learning

Active informal learning is learning that takes place at work or in work-related environments. This approach is mostly used on jobs that require continuous learning and development. Individuals use this approach to respond to strong learning demands in organizations that have a robust learning culture. Knowledge acquired can easily be applied to an individual's job or work. Examples include working on challenging assignments, working with individuals who are more knowledgeable, and attending leadership forums where company leaders or executives facilitate discussion on specific topics.[7] Active informal learning is most useful to organizations.

Autonomous Informal Learning

Autonomous informal learning refers to learning that takes place outside of the work environment. This approach is mostly used by individuals with a strong motivation to learn and who are willing to invest time in learning about a specific topic. Examples include using the Internet to research a particular topic or participating in an online community to learn about an issue. Topics can include exploring a new career or a work-related issue.

Spontaneous Informal Learning

This type of informal learning is unintentional and occurs at work. In spontaneous informal learning situations, an individual is not actively seeking new knowledge. Learning is mostly a by-product of engaging in some type of work activity. Examples include learning from daily interactions with colleagues, customers, or other individuals at work. These interactions can be virtual or face-to-face.

Passive Informal Learning

This is the simplest type of informal learning and it is very similar to spontaneous informal learning; however, it occurs outside of work. Passive informal learning occurs through daily social interactions with peers and other knowledgeable people. In passive informal learning situations, the person is not actively seeking new knowledge, and whatever is imparted might or might not be absorbed and integrated into the person's existing knowledge base.

The preceding four-type categorization of informal learning has implications for the learning function in that the activity or activities required for learning vary depending on the type of informal learning. The following is a list of selected activities that can result in informal learning,[8] and Table 5.1 highlights activities associated with each type of informal learning:

- Using electronic mail
- Searching the Internet for information
- Using an Intranet (such as company-specific networks)
- Participating in forums
- Mentoring other people
- Coaching other people
- Attending conferences
- Attending business-sponsored lunches
- Working and interacting with colleagues
- Using on-the-job experiences (This is a large area and learning depends on the type of job experience. Examples include job rotation, stretch assignments, and so on.)
- Working in teams/groups
- Interacting/working with customers
- Creating professional social networking (for example, LinkedIn)
- Blogging
- Watching TV/movies/videos
- Playing video games
- Using private social networking (such as Facebook)
- Reading books, journals, articles, and so on

Table 5.1 Type of Informal Learning and Work/Nonwork Activity

Work and Nonwork Activity	Active°	Autonomous	Spontaneous°	Passive
Electronic mail	✓	✓	✓	✓
Internet (searching for information)	✓	✓	✓	✓
Intranet (for example, company-specific networks)	✓		✓	
Participating in forums	✓		✓	
Mentoring other people	✓		✓	
Coaching other people	✓		✓	
Attending conferences	✓		✓	
Attending business-sponsored lunches	✓		✓	
Working and interacting with colleagues	✓		✓	
On-the-job experiences	✓		✓	
Working in teams/groups	✓		✓	
Interacting/ working with customers	✓		✓	
Professional social networking (for example, LinkedIn)	✓		✓	
Blogging		✓		✓

Work and Nonwork Activity	Active°	Autonomous	Spontaneous°	Passive
Watching TV/ movies/videos		✓		✓
Playing video games		✓		✓
Private social networking (for example, Facebook)		✓	✓	
Reading books, journals, articles, and so on	✓	✓	✓	✓

* It must be stressed here that activities in both the active and spontaneous informal learning categories are the same. However, an important difference between active informal learning and spontaneous informal learning is the individual's intention, which is much greater in active informal learning.

Informal Learning Strategy

An organization's informal learning strategy has to be developed with care, as too much guidance and structure will result in formalized learning. Informal learning is intuitively counter to formal learning.

Informal learning strategy refers to the *activities, learning capability,* and *incentives* used to manage the informal learning process in an organization:

- **Informal learning activities:** These are the activities that provide employees with opportunities to learn. Table 5.1 provides a sample list of activities.

- **Learning capability:** This refers to the ability of each employee to learn from experience or the activities referred to in Table 5.1. For example, do employees need to learn "how to learn"?

- **Incentives:** This refers to enticements in place to encourage employees to participate in informal learning.

An important question here is whether to have a strategy for each type of informal learning activity, referred to in Table 5.1, or a general strategy that covers all four types of informal learning. The reality is that each of the four types of informal learning calls for different types of activities. However, from a learning perspective, active informal learning is the most relevant to organizations, as they have more control over this type of learning relative to the other three types. So, the focus of organizations is on active informal learning.

Broad Issues to Consider When Developing an Informal Learning Strategy

Perhaps the most important factor to keep in mind is that informal learning strategy differs for each organization depending on several factors and issues that need to be considered when developing the strategy:

- Informal learning *complements* formalized learning. However, by itself, informal learning can be precarious because learning outcomes cannot be determined or predicted. Moreover, informal learning needs to be part of a larger "blended approach" to content delivery.[9] One way informal learning can be blended with other types of learning is to teach required knowledge through formalized learning and allow each individual to use a learning method of his choice from a variety of possible sources to learn nonrequired knowledge.[10]

- Informal learning is *industry-specific*. Industries such as financial, health care, and insurance are heavily regulated by the federal government and states in terms of how confidential information is protected, stored, and shared. Organizations in these industries have to limit what their employees can discuss, share, and access in a work context.[11] In contrast, organizations in relatively less-regulated industries, such as consumer products, manufacturing, education, and retail, have more flexibility in terms of information sharing and knowledge management.

- There are *limitations to informal learning*. Informal learning is more likely to increase knowledge (cognitive changes) than change individual behavior (behavioral changes). (See Chapter 2, "Adult Learning and Development.")

- The *outcome of informal learning is mostly tacit knowledge*, which is extremely useful, but difficult to transfer and share with others.[12] (See Chapter 3, "The Art of Knowledge Acquisition.")

- Informal learning can work well when *employees have autonomy* in their work and the organization has a culture that promotes creativity, entrepreneurship, and learning, as well as facilitates communication among individuals.

Specific Questions to Consider When Developing an Informal Learning Strategy

In addition to the broad issues in the preceding section, an organization should consider the following when crafting an effective informal learning strategy:

- To what extent should we focus on activities that facilitate interaction among employees? These activities can be onsite or offsite social activities.

- To what extent should we encourage and monitor online discussions and connection through social media?

- To what extent should we make information gathering and sharing an important part of managers' jobs?

- To what extent should we encourage mentor and mentee relationships, especially between experts and novices?

- To what extent should we provide guidance on how to find information, conduct research, and share information with others?

- To what extent should we help employees understand the causes and symptoms of information overload and, more important, how to prevent information overload?

- To what extent should we develop programs that improve visual literacy (the ability to learn from images and videos) among employees and managers?

- To what extent should we use asynchronous online learning methods to facilitate informal learning?

Who Is Most Likely to Participate in Informal Learning?

Informal learning cannot be formally evaluated and this can be risky in terms of the quality of learning that results from informal learning activities. It is important to understand which individuals will benefit most from informal learning. In other words, informal learning is more effective when individuals have the requisite individual characteristics.

Chapter 6, "Customized Learning and Learner Control (Trend 3)," discusses several individual traits and characteristics that can affect learning, but in the context of informal learning there are a few characteristics that can facilitate this type of learning. They include motivation to learn (for example, willingness to seek learning opportunities), internal locus of control (such as belief in one's control over learning outcomes), learning goal orientation (for instance, willingness to improve competency in specific areas), and feedback orientation (for example, actively seeking feedback to improve performance or enhance knowledge).[14]

The personality traits of extroversion and openness to experience can also affect informal learning. These two traits predispose individuals to establish interpersonal relationships with others at work and outside of work.

In addition, employees need to have the competencies to learn from experience. This can include

- Learning agility (see Chapter 9, "Extreme Development: Stretch Assignments and Learning Agility (Trend 6)")
- Relevant prior knowledge
- Visual literacy

Summary

This chapter began by describing four different types of informal learning, as referred to in Figure 5.1. Each type of informal learning has its own specific activities. Following this, the chapter provided an in-depth look at an organization's informal learning strategy, which is conceptualized as activities, learning capability, and incentives used to manage the informal learning process in an organization. The chapter then discussed the characteristics of individuals most likely to benefit most from informal learning. Overall, as workplace learning shifts from the traditional model of instructor-led to more learner-centered, focus on informal learning will remain sharp.[14]

6

Customized Learning and Learner Control (Trend 3)

What's in this chapter:

- What is customized learning?
- Different types of instructional design
- Individual characteristics
- Learner control

As mentioned in Chapter 1, "Forces Shaping the Corporate Learning Function," the learning and development industry in the United States is a multibillion dollar industry.[1] Every year, numerous individuals participate in learning activities for the purpose of developing competence. The assumption is that acquired competencies help organizations increase efficiency and improve competitiveness. But does the outcome of learning activities depend on context (for example, learning environment and instructional design)? This is an important question to examine if you are to understand the effect of training or development on employee learning and performance.

Despite the plethora of research and findings advocating the use of learning activities in organizations, there is one major concern: Everyone does not benefit equally from learning activities. Moreover, the fact that people benefit differently and sometimes not at all from the same training or development experiences is ignored.[2]

Trend 3 suggests that learning has to be customized with the learner having considerable control. That is the focus of this chapter.

What Is Customized Learning?

Customized learning in this chapter refers to learning that is tailored to the unique characteristics of the learner or learners. This point is important because learning can be customized for one individual or a group (individuals with similar characteristics).

The idea of customization is based on an academic concept—aptitude treatment interaction[3]—which suggests that some instructional designs (for example, developmental experiences) and individual attributes will interact differently. Essentially, an individual will respond differently to instructional design based on his or her specific characteristics.[4] Further, this means that the effectiveness of a specific learning activity depends on the appropriate "fit" between instructional design and individual characteristics.[5] Figure 6.1 illustrates this notion of "fit."

Different Types of Instructional Design

Instructional design includes several components that work together to provide a complete learning experience. The top part of Figure 6.1 shows the two most important components that can be customized: *instructional methods* to deliver instructional content and *sequencing of learning activities*.

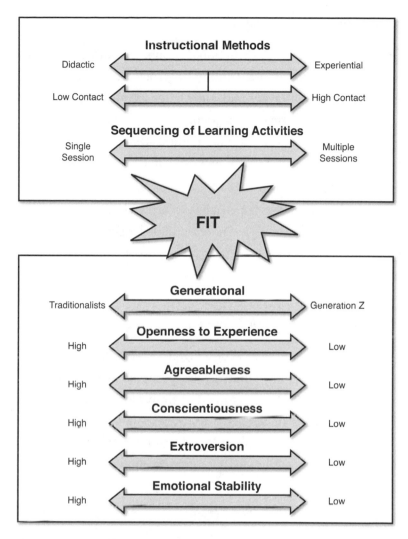

Figure 6.1 (Top) Example of instructional design components; (Bottom) Examples of individual characteristics

Instructional methods can take two broad approaches:

- Didactic versus experiential
- Low contact versus high contact

Didactic Versus Experiential[6]

A didactic approach to instructional design takes the traditional form of learning (for example, from an instructor to a learner) and focuses on information giving and knowledge acquisition. The goal of this approach is to bring about a cognitive change (for example, increase in knowledge). Instructional methods that use this approach include lectures, seminars, reading material, and discussions.

An experiential approach, in contrast, focuses on learning through experiences. The goal of this approach is to bring about cognitive and behavioral changes (for example, increase knowledge and skill acquisition). Instructional methods utilizing this approach include immersion programs, workshops, and role-plays.

Low Contact Versus High Contact[7]

Instructional methods can be visualized on a continuum in terms of the interpersonal contact that occurs between learners and the instructor or among the learners ranging from low-contact activities or experiences to high-contact activities or experiences. Low-contact methods include asynchronous online learning and videos. High-contact methods include team learning and group discussions.

Sequencing of Learning Activities

Along with the issue of instructional design, how learning activities are sequenced can influence learning. Learning instruction can be conducted at different times (for example, learning activities are distributed over several sessions) or conducted in one session. Usually, this is determined by the complexity of the learning material.[8] Complex concepts can be broken down into modules and taught incrementally over several sessions, making it easier for learners to absorb complex material.

It is important to remember that the appropriate sequencing of learning activities (either one session or multiple sessions) is determined by the complexity of the instructional content and the learner's needs and characteristics.

Individual Characteristics

The bottom image in Figure 6.1 shows a few of the individual characteristics that have the potential to interact with instructional design. They include age (as reflected by generational differences or generational types) and personality (as reflected by the big five personality traits).[9] These were briefly discussed in Chapter 2, "Adult Learning and Development."

Before describing individual characteristics, it is important to see how the interaction between individual characteristics and instructional design occurs. As the bottom of Figure 6.1 illustrates, there are various types of interactions. Four examples include

- Instructional methods interacting with personality traits
- Sequencing of learning activities interacting with personality traits
- Instructional methods interacting with generational type
- Sequencing of learning activities interacting with generational type

Generational Differences and Learning

As discussed in Chapter 1, there are five generations:

- **Traditionalists** (born between 1922 and 1945): 68–86 years old
- **Baby boomers** (born between 1946 and 1964): 49–67 years old

- **Generation X** (born between 1965 and 1980): 33–48 years old
- **Generation Y or millennials** (born between 1981 and 2000): 13–32 years old
- **Generation Z** (born after 2000): 14 years and younger

Each generation has specific attitudes toward learning and learning styles.

Traditionalists (born between 1922 and 1945) are loyal and committed to their employers. They believe careers should be built around working for one or two employers.

They prefer:

- Instructor-led teaching (They expect leadership from the instructor.)
- Face-to-face or traditional learning environments
- Less usage of technology-based learning
- Didactic instructional methods with considerable emphasis on reading and lectures
- To learn from subject matter experts

Because they possess a vast amount of knowledge and experience, traditionalists have the potential to become excellent mentors and coaches. They are good listeners.

*Baby boom*ers (born between 1946 and 1964) believe in achieving success through hard work. They have a "live-to-work"[10] approach toward life. They are less conservative than traditionalists, but they still believe that careers should be built around working at only one or two organizations throughout their career. (This is more true for late baby boomers born between 1960 and 1964.)

They prefer:

- Instructor-led teaching, but are not hesitant to ask questions or question authority
- Traditional face-to-face learning environments, but are also comfortable with learning in teams[11]
- A linear approach to content delivery where the sequence is well structured and logical[12]
- Content that is text-heavy[13] (for example, uses more text than graphics)
- Learning that is rewarded[14] and tied to career success

Similar to traditionalists, baby boomers are good mentors and coaches.

Generation X (born between 1965 and 1980) is less loyal and less committed to their employers than baby boomers, but they have stable career progression. Job security is important to them. They are more self-dependent in managing their careers and job transitions. Further, they believe that career growth through development is important.

They prefer:

- Hybrid or blended approaches to learning (for example, learning environments that have a mix of online and traditional face-to-face instructional methods)
- Having control over their learning[15] (for instance, how they learn, where they learn, and when they learn)
- Instruction content that is customized to suit their needs
- Technology-based learning that is not complex and that is easy to use[16]

- Learning that is pragmatic and can be applied to different situations[17]
- Mentors, coaches,[18] and learning on the job (for example, experiential learning)

Generation Y or millennials (born between 1981 and 2000) have little or no commitment to their employers. They are more committed to their careers and believe a successful career requires moving across several jobs and organizations. They use technology as a language to manage their work, jobs, and careers.

They prefer:

- Technology-based learning that is informal and allows extensive learner control
- Learning methods that allow virtual and social collaboration
- Learning through games, graphics, and videos
- The instructor to be a facilitator in the learning process
- Mobile learning that allows them to learn anywhere, anytime
- Regular and constructive feedback in real time
- Learning that is quick and concise

The Big Five Personality Traits

Personality is generally defined as individual differences or specific traits that predispose people to think, feel, and behave in certain ways.[19] A person can have many personality traits, but the *big five personality traits* are known to be related to learning and performance outcomes.[20]

The big five personality traits include[21]

- Openness to experience
- Agreeableness

- Conscientiousness
- Extroversion
- Emotional stability

The big five personality traits can impact motivation to learn and how an individual acquires, retains, and reproduces learned capabilities.[22]

Openness to Experience

This personality trait refers to the extent to which an individual is original, intellectual, curious, creative, imaginative, and conventional.[23] Individuals high on openness to experience are open to change, curious about new surroundings or environments, willing to take risks, and willing to explore new opportunities and experiences.[24] They are also more likely to adapt to new environments and situations; in addition, they establish interpersonal relationships with people from a variety of cultural backgrounds.[25]

From a learning perspective, individuals high on openness to experience may prefer learning environments that provide considerable control over the learning process and the autonomy to discover or explore instructional content that is important to them.[26]

Agreeableness

This personality trait describes the extent to which someone is cooperative, sociable, forgiving, tolerant, and argumentative.[27] Individuals high on agreeableness seek mutual understanding, are less competitive, and are committed to forming interpersonal relationships and mutually beneficial partnerships.[28]

As far as learning is concerned, individuals high on agreeableness are suited for learning environments that emphasize teamwork and collaboration among learners.

Conscientiousness

This personality trait describes the degree to which an individual is purposeful, hardworking, organized, dependable, and self-disciplined.[29] Out of the big five personality traits, conscientiousness is related to performance across a range of job types.[30] Individuals high on conscientiousness are likely to have strong goals, high motivation to learn, and increased motivation to use learned competencies.[31] Further, these individuals are willing to invest considerable effort into learning new skills and behaviors.[32] Overall, conscientious individuals are more likely to retain and reproduce learned skills and behaviors.

This personality trait is probably helpful in all learning environments but is extremely useful in learning environments that require the learner to work independently.

Extroversion

This personality trait refers to the extent to which an individual is sociable, active, talkative, fun loving, and affectionate.[33] Individuals who are high on extroversion are more likely to engage in social activities that involve interpersonal relationships.[34] These individuals can establish interpersonal relationships with people from a variety of backgrounds, and more important, learn from interpersonal interactions.[35]

In learning environments, especially in technology-based environments, individuals high on extroversion may prefer instructional methods that involve extensive interpersonal interactions.[36] Introverts may prefer instructional methods that allow independent learning (for example, working alone).

Emotional Stability

This personality trait describes individuals in terms of anxiety, calmness, self-confidence, worry, insecurity, and nervousness.[37] An individual who is high on emotional stability is more likely to manage and tolerate stressful situations or conditions. Emotional stability can affect an individual's ability to form interpersonal relationships or engage in interpersonal interactions.[38]

From a learning perspective, individuals low on emotional stability may find extreme developmental practices (see Chapter 9, "Extreme Development: Stretch Assignments and Learning Agility"), such as stretch assignments, uncomfortable and stressful.

In addition to the big five personality traits, one individual trait that is considered essential in terms of learning is *goal orientation*. This concept describes the goal(s) an individual has in a learning environment.[39] Goal orientation can be segmented into two categories:

• Learning goal orientation

• Performance goal orientation

Learning goal orientation describes the extent to which an individual concentrates on acquiring or mastering competencies. Individuals with learning goal orientation focus more on increasing or improving competence, relative to performance. In contrast, performance goal orientation focuses on the extent to which an individual prefers high performance and favorable evaluation by others. Individuals with performance goal orientation emphasize performance over learning.[40] In general, learning goal orientation is associated with expending greater effort in learning environments.

Learner Control

The idea of customization of learning is appealing; however, it can be expensive to customize learning environments for individuals or specific groups of individuals with similar characteristics.

One way to customize learning is to allow the learner more control over the learning process. That is, the learner can decide how to learn (method), when to learn (timing), what to learn (content), where to learn (location), and how much to learn (practice).[41] This is referred to as *learner control.*[42]

With greater control, learners can more actively tailor training to meet their own changing needs. It is suggested that more actively engaging learners during training leads them to learn the deeper, structural elements of a task more effectively.[43] Examples of high-level learner control include the trainee's choice of what instructional content to view, the order and pace at which to view this content, whether to complete optional quizzes to assess personal learning progress, and the nature and amount of feedback received during the program. With high learner control, decisions to use (or not use) learner control features, and the extent of their use, are at the discretion of the trainee.[44]

Learner control is especially important in technology-based learning environments[45] where the learner is separated from the instructor by distance.[46] In addition, individuals high on openness to experience and extroversion are more likely to benefit from learning environments that allow greater learning control.[47] Essentially, all learners should have some control over their learning process.[48]

Summary

This chapter focused on the discussion that learning has to be customized with the learner having considerable control over the learning process. The first part of this chapter described customized learning, which refers to learning that is tailored to the unique characteristics of the learner or learners. More specifically, for learning to be effective, there has to be a "fit" between instructional design and individual characteristics. The chapter then described different types of instructional designs in terms of important components that can be customized: instructional methods to deliver instructional content and sequencing of learning activities. This was followed by identifying a few of the individual characteristics that have the potential to interact with instructional design; these include age and personality. Finally, the chapter closed with a discussion on the notion of learner control.

7

Continuous Learning (Trend 4)

What's in this chapter:

- What is continuous learning?
- Reasons for continuous learning
- Strategies for organizations
- Strategies for the individual

It is obvious that learning is important. As discussed earlier in the book, corporate learning and development is a means to an end for the organization and for the individual. Presently, a major concern is that there actually is no concrete "end" in today's learning culture. Traditionally, adult learning had an endpoint, such as an educational degree, diploma, or professional certification. After earning a degree or credential, formal learning ended, and any additional learning was optional. This has changed. As discussed in Chapter 1, "Forces Shaping the Corporate Learning Function," we are expected to learn all the time, formally and informally, to meet the challenges of a changing work environment. Each of us is now a 24/7 learner!

This chapter discusses the fourth trend of continuous learning.

What Is Continuous Learning?

Continuous learning occurs at three levels—organizational, group, and individual—but the starting point is the individual level. In this chapter, continuous learning refers to the process in which an individual participates to acquire new knowledge at work and outside of work on an ongoing basis.[1] This includes formal and informal learning.

Continuous learning can be categorized into three types: adaptive, generative, and transformative:[2]

- **Adaptive learning:** This type of learning occurs when the individual *reacts* to environmental challenges and demands, such as new job responsibilities. Here, the individual has control over his or her learning process.

- **Generative learning:** This type of learning occurs when the individual is *proactive* in increasing or improving his or her competencies in expectation of future changes that may occur at work. These changes may include a promotion or a new assignment that requires a move to a different country.

- **Transformative learning:** This type of learning occurs when an individual *considers* changing his or her job or career to pursue a new field or direction. An important point here is that this type of learning is not directly related to the individual's current job.

Reasons for Continuous Learning

Individuals commit themselves to continuous learning for a variety of reasons, some of which include the following:

- **The employer-employee relationship is changing:** As discussed in Chapter 1, the employer-employee relationship is evolving to one in which the employee assumes control over his learning and career. The employee is the architect of his or her learning, and learning is positively related to career success.

The extent to which an employee can adapt to changing job requirements, seek new career opportunities within his or her current place of employment or change jobs is highly dependent on continuously maintaining current competencies and acquiring new competencies. Continuous learning allows individuals to increase their value to their employer and improve their employability and marketability in the job market.[3]

• **Learning is an essential part of work:** Most jobs today have an element of learning embedded in work activities. Learning can precede work assignments or occur while an individual is engaged in work activities. In addition, jobs require participating in virtual teams, joining business-related social networks (virtual or face-to-face social networks), working remotely, and having and using technological knowledge.[4] These characteristics require learning on an ongoing basis.

• **Jobs require teamwork:** Working in groups or in teams is a requirement for most jobs. Individuals have to be trained or developed to work in teams, and they need to continuously learn about collaboration, cooperation, sharing knowledge, and working toward a common goal. Team or group members who don't learn to work well together will find it challenging to survive in today's high-performance, team-based organizational culture.[5]

Strategies for Organizations

An important aspect of continuous learning is that it helps organizations attract, retain, and develop talent.[6] To a large extent, this relates to organizational culture. Organizations can develop a *culture of continuous learning* by transforming into a *learning organization*.[7]

What is a culture of continuous learning? A culture of continuous learning is one in which employees are encouraged and rewarded to learn, develop, and grow. There are specific policies, practices, and employee behaviors and attitudes that contribute to the formation of a continuous learning culture:

- Individuals are aware of their learning needs and are responsible for acquiring, retaining, and maintaining their competencies to meet their learning needs.

- Individuals are provided with opportunities (for example, work assignments) to use and apply what they have learned.[8]

- Individuals have a strong willingness to participate in learning activities.

- Individuals are assigned mentors to address any performance deficiencies.

- Supervisors and managers support learning and encourage their subordinates to participate in learning and development activities.[9]

- Creativity is encouraged and valued; learning is provided to support the implementation of new ideas.[10]

- Learning programs and activities are customized to suit the individual's learning needs.

- There is considerable focus on team learning.[11]

- High potential employees are placed in fast-track developmental programs (for example, stretch assignments and leadership development) to prepare them for future roles and responsibilities.

- Leaders and top management are extremely supportive of learning.

- There is a dedicated talent management department that works closely with HR and other parts of the organization.

- There are clear career paths, and professional development is offered to support career development.

- Informal learning is encouraged and appreciated.

- A blended approach to technology-based learning that combines the right mix of mobile learning, social learning, online learning technology, gaming, and traditional face-to-face learning is used.

- Learning management systems are constantly updated to meet the changing learning needs of employees.

- Performance and learning metrics are used to evaluate and improve learning.

It is important to emphasize that a continuous learning culture takes time to develop. It is critical that employees are provided with resources and opportunities to learn. Building a culture of continuous learning requires support from top management, managers, and employees to have a positive attitude toward learning, resources to provide learning, and jobs that provide the opportunities to use learning.

A *culture of continuous learning* can be part of a *learning organization*. The term *learning organization*[12] is assigned to an organization that has the capability to use learning as a source of competitive advantage by implementing processes and practices that allow employees to learn, develop, and grow. As a result of having a highly skilled workforce, the organization can create, sustain, and remain competitive in the changing business environment.

From an HR perspective, a learning organization has five core characteristics:

- The learning function is closely aligned with business goals and objectives; it is also constantly evolving and adjusting to changing requirements.

- A corporate university or a similar, centralized unit that is dedicated to learning provides continuous learning to all important stakeholders.

- Learning systems (see Chapter 11, "Investment in Workforce Learning and Development") are used not only to train and develop employees, but also to create, acquire, store, and disseminate knowledge across the organization.

- A strong culture of continuous learning sends a clear message to all important stakeholders that employee learning and development are encouraged and rewarded.

- Technology is embedded in all aspects of learning processes from designing programs to creating and transferring knowledge.

Strategies for the Individual

An important question is: How does an individual become a continuous learner? A continuous learner can be defined as someone who willingly participates in learning activities on an ongoing basis to acquire and maintain career-related competencies.[13] Learning activities can include formal and informal learning activities.

"Willingness to participate in learning"[14] is an important concept to understand. What encourages people to participate in learning and what are some important outcomes of participation? First, willingness to participate in learning can be separated into two categories:

- Willingness to participate in training activities
- Willingness to participate in development activities

Second, similar to what was mentioned in Chapter 1, willingness to participate in training activities focuses more on competencies needed on a current job, whereas willingness to participate in development activities focuses more on competencies needed in future roles. This is discussed more in Chapter 9, "Extreme Development: Stretch Assignments and Learning Agility (Trend 6)."

Third, several factors can affect an individual's willingness to participate in training and development activities. It is important to keep in mind that specific factors can affect both (training and development) differently. A few of these factors exist at the organizational or learning systems level (for example, practices and activities) and others exist at the individual level (for example, personal traits). Some of the important factors include[15]

Organizational/Learning Systems Level

- Culture of continuous learning
- Individualized career development plans
- Having mentors who are experts[16]
- Continued or regular performance feedback from supervisors
- Supervisors' encouragement and support for learning[17]
- Need for continued certification and education requirements[18]
- Type of work (for example, technology or knowledge intensive)[19]
- Involvement with work (for example, passion, and engagement)[20]
- Stage of career development (for example, early career, midcareer, and late career)[21]

Individual Level

- Attitude toward development (for example, how enjoyable and worthwhile is development?)[22]
- Environmental scanning abilities (for example, how aware is the individual about her profession and career opportunities/threats that exist in the profession?)
- Motivation to learn (for example, intrinsic motivation)[23]

- Internal locus of control (for example, the belief that an individual controls her career growth)[24]
- The big five personality traits (for example, openness to experience and extroversion)[25]

Whether a factor (mentioned previously) positively or negatively affects continuous learning depends on context. However, one point is clear: Continuous learning has significant outcomes. Individuals who participate in continuous learning are more satisfied with their jobs and more committed to their respective organizations.[26]

Summary

This chapter focused on continuous learning, which occurs at three levels: organizational, group, and individual. As described in this chapter, continuous learning can be categorized into three types: adaptive, generative, and transformative. The chapter discussed the reasons for continuous learning and why individuals commit to continuous learning. Then the chapter described strategies that organizations can use to facilitate continuous learning. This can be done by developing a culture of continuous learning and becoming a learning organization. Finally, the chapter discussed strategies for the individual to become a continuous learner.

8

Learning and Development Through Teamwork (Trend 5)

What's in this chapter:

- Different types of teams and how teams work
- Successful teams and effective team members
- The importance of collaborative learning

If you search online for "future of work" and read what various scholars, authors, HR professionals, and users say about their experiences and predictions, you will discover the "future of work" is similar to acting in a play or a movie.[1] Moreover, work is project-based. Employees come from different places with different competencies, motivation, and goals. Each person plays (does) his part and moves on to the next project. Collaboration is essential and teamwork is a critical part of work.

As discussed in Chapter 1, "Forces Shaping the Corporate Learning Function," work today is becoming complex, requiring individuals to collaborate with more than one person or several people on the same project or assignment. Similar to what will occur in the future, the current structure of work requires coordination among individuals with diverse backgrounds and competencies. Working in teams is now a norm in many organizations—it is the rule, not the exception. Individuals have to learn how to successfully work in teams and learn from their teammates. This chapter focuses on development and learning through teamwork (Trend 5).

Different Types of Teams and How Teams Work

A team develops when two or more people collaborate to work toward a common goal or goals. Three important goals include

- **Manage the flow of knowledge within the organization:**[2] Team members acquire, transfer, share, and retain knowledge.

- **Learn from one other:** Individuals from a wide variety of backgrounds and with complementary competencies work together.[3]

- **Solve complex problems:**[4] Individuals work together on tasks or complete tasks that would be difficult for one person to complete alone.[5]

There are several types of team combinations, but before describing the different types, it is important to understand how teams are formed.

Formal teams go through five stages of development:[6]

- **Forming:** During this stage, team members get to know one another and establish guidelines and rules for working as a group. They may appoint a group leader at this stage.

- **Storming:** At this stage, team members form doubts about one another. There are conflicts among team members; each member can feel frustrated and dissatisfied.

- **Norming:** During this stage, team members develop shared goals for functioning over a long period of time. They accept one another and cope with any differences. There is team cohesion and a willingness to collaborate.

- **Performing:** Team members work on the actual assignments or tasks they were convened to complete or perform. They function and work well together to achieve the overarching goal.

- **Adjourning:** This stage involves team members disbanding at the completion of a task or project. The team can reflect on its experiences and challenges and make plans for future collaborations.

From a learning perspective, the norming and performing stages can involve team members learning from one another.

As mentioned earlier, there are different types of teams, each one having its unique characteristics and features.

Cross-Functional Teams

These types of teams include individuals from different departments and functional units collaborating to work on a specific task. Team members can have different competencies and experiences that facilitate innovation and creativity. Cross-functional teams are becoming popular in today's workplace because people are increasingly required to work across departments and functions. Team members can learn about new areas and topics, diversity, and how to interact with people from different backgrounds.

Self-Managed Teams or Self-Directed Teams

These types of teams are responsible for producing or managing an entire product or service. They include members who have the autonomy to make decisions, manage themselves, and determine how best to get the job done. In addition, these types of teams have the autonomy to set their own goals, make decisions, and select and remove members.[7] Usually self-managed or self-directed teams work on projects that are complex; this requires experts from a variety of backgrounds.

Problem-Solving Teams[8]

These types of teams include members who are volunteers from a variety of departments and functions. They come together or collaborate to work on specific problems or issues. Most of the time, this type of team is formed for a short period of time and disbands after solving the specific problems or issues.[9]

Virtual Teams

Members of virtual teams are geographically separated and communicate through technology, such as computers and the Internet. These teams are difficult to manage because most of the time they have fewer synchronous sessions and depend on virtual communication and interactions. Virtual teams are becoming popular because they help organizations lower cost by reducing travel time and allowing individuals from different areas to work together.

Cross-Border Teams or Multicultural Teams[10]

Individuals in cross-border or multicultural teams come from different geographic locations, countries, and cultures. They can speak different languages and normally they work across different time zones. These teams are similar to "virtual" teams in terms of their characteristics and structure (for example, most of the interactions and work is conducted using technologies such as e-mail, Internet, and video).[11]

Multicultural teams are becoming increasingly prevalent in international organizations operating in a wide variety of industries. As such, there are certain best practices that enable multicultural teams to work well:[12]

- Team members should have strong communication skills and virtual team skills.

- Team members should have cross-cultural focused competencies.
- Team leaders should be identified early in the team formation process.
- Goals should be clear with well-stated project targets and deadlines.
- Team members should network with one another using electronic social networks to build trust and communication.
- Teams should continuously be monitored to detect any obstacles to virtual collaboration. Issues or challenges have to be resolved quickly. When and where possible, the team should have access to mentors who can help them manage cross-cultural problems and misunderstandings.

As more organizations use multicultural teams, especially virtual teams to work on projects or address issues, knowledge about how teams work and how to make teams more effective becomes critical for managers as they prepare employees for a variety of team experiences.

Successful Teams and Effective Team Members

Successful teams have specific characteristics. The eight dimensions developed by Cannon-Bowers, Tannenbaum, Salas, and Volpe provide a picture of what a successful team would look like:[13]

- **Adaptability:** Team members need to have the flexibility to adjust and adapt to new or changing circumstances that can occur within the team environment.
- **Shared situational awareness:** Team members need to share unique information or knowledge with one another.

- **Performance monitoring and feedback:** Team members need to monitor the team's performance and also seek and provide feedback.

- **Team management:** Team members need to plan, assign duties and responsibilities, and motivate one another.

- **Interpersonal relations:** Team members should cooperatively interact with one another to resolve conflicts.

- **Coordination:** Team members should coordinate work and organize team resources in a way that allows them to complete assignments and activities successfully and in a timely manner.

- **Communication:** Team members should communicate clearly with one another and share information effectively and efficiently.

- **Decision making:** Team members should make decisions based on a thorough process that involves assessing the problem, evaluating various solutions, and examining the various consequences of the solution.

In addition to team characteristics, a good team member should demonstrate certain individual characteristics or traits. Some of the characteristics include the following:

- A team member has to be *dependable* and trustworthy.[14]

- A team member has to be *flexible* in a variety of work environments.[15]

- A team member has to be a *good problem solver.*[16]

- A team member has to be a *good listener.*[17]

- A team member has to *participate actively* in team projects and assignments.[18]

The reality is that teams do malfunction for a variety of reasons. Lencioni's model of dysfunctional teams[19] has been widely used to identify problems teams may have:

- **There is absence of trust:** Team members have to be comfortable with one another and should not be reluctant to admit their weaknesses and mistakes.

- **There is fear of conflict:** Team members should have passionate, open discussion about important issues and should avoid concealing or hiding important topics that need to be discussed.

- **There is lack of commitment:** Team members should have clear direction and a strong commitment to a plan of action.

- **There is avoidance of accountability:** Team members should hold one another responsible for committing to a plan of action.

- **There is inattention to results:** Team members should focus on collective goals and objectives more than individual achievements and ego.

In addition, there are recognized barriers that serve as obstacles to teams functioning properly. They include no clear identity and purpose established at the outset, nonexistent team leadership, and poor communication among team members.[20]

The Importance of Collaborative Learning

Collaborative learning refers to learning that occurs when people work together on specific projects or tasks. Collaborative learning in teams has two important components:

- Team members have to learn how to work in a team.
- Team members have to learn from the team's experiences.

Learning how to work in a team is reflected in the ideas discussed earlier in this chapter. How teams learn from a team experience is slightly more complex.

A team experience involves the creation of knowledge that is collective in nature. It is dependent on how team members work together.[21] Each member makes a unique contribution but has a synergistic effect[22] when collaborating with team members. This results in collective knowledge being greater than individual knowledge (for example, similar to "the whole is greater than the sum of its parts").

The extent to which teams learn depends on

- How well team members share new ideas and knowledge with one another[23]

- The extent to which team members challenge one another on important issues and provide constructive feedback[24]

- The ability of team members to work together effectively[25]

- The extent of face-to-face and virtual interactions among team members[26]

- How well knowledge is transferred from one team member to another[27]

- The ability of team members to learn from mistakes[28]

Team learning results in three types of group learning outcomes:[29]

- **Adaptive group learning:** This type of learning occurs when team members react to an event or stimuli and make small adjustments, such as determining how team members will learn or share information.[30]

- **Generative group learning:** This form of learning takes place when team members proactively and deliberately learn by participating in group activities that provide new knowledge (for example, discussions).[31]

- **Transformative group learning:** This category of learning occurs when group members modify, change, or alter the way the team works or learns.[32]

Finally, there are specific instructional methods that depend on a team structure to create a learning environment. These include

- Cross-training[33]
- Simulations[34]
- Action teams[35]

These instructional methods can be used to increase team learning.

Summary

This chapter provided an introduction to how learning and development occur through teamwork. It began by describing how teams are formed and the different types of teams such as cross-functional teams, self-managed teams, problem solving teams, virtual teams, and cross-border teams. The chapter argued that successful teams have certain characteristics and described these characteristics. The chapter closed with a discussion on the importance of collaborative learning, with an emphasis on two important components needed for collaborative learning: Team members have to learn how to work in a team, and team members have to learn from the team's experiences.

9

Extreme Development: Stretch Assignments and Learning Agility (Trend 6)

What's in this chapter:

- What is development?
- What is extreme development?
- The importance of stretch assignments
- The importance of learning agility

As mentioned previously, development is different from training. Both bring about a permanent change in competencies; training focuses on competencies that are needed in the current job, whereas development focuses on competencies that are needed in the short or long term. From an organizational perspective, the main goal of development is to identify talent challenges (for example, talent shortages) that the organization will face in the future while also enhancing the competencies needed to address those challenges. In addition, development allows organizations to

- Increase employee retention (employees become more valuable to the organization after development)
- Increase employee motivation, engagement, and loyalty
- Effectively manage staffing deficiencies by developing existing employees

Development enables employees to

- Concentrate on their strengths and simultaneously overcome their weaknesses

- Address their developmental needs and prevent skills obsolescence

- Take charge of their own careers to remain competitive in today's global workforce

This chapter discusses the sixth trend: extreme development.

What Is Development?

As mentioned in Chapter 7, "Continuous Learning (Trend 4)," today's workers are extremely busy, overworked, stressed, and cognitively overloaded. Development takes time, effort, and resources. For employees, development has become a means to an end, and there has to be a positive rate of return on the time invested in the learning process. Learning has to lead to something that is valuable, and what is considered valuable is different to different individuals. In this context, it is important to understand an individual's *willingness to participate in development activities,*[1] which refers to an individual's attitude and motivation toward development. A variety of factors can influence willingness to participate in development activities, such as organizational and job tenure, age, prior development, and so on,[2] but the value-added factor is critical. Learning through development has to add value to an individual's career progression and goals.

Types of Development Practices

The type of practice that is used to develop an individual makes a huge difference in whether learning occurs and at what level. Organizations use a variety of activities or practices to develop employees. Table 9.1 lists the most popular practices.

Table 9.1 Development Practices

Development Practice	Description
Formal university coursework	A structured and formal coursework leads to a graduate degree or a certificate, such as an executive-level MBA.
Assessment centers	This process evaluates and assesses candidates on a variety of topics with the goal of providing developmental feedback. This process can take place in a specific location that can be offsite or onsite.
On-the-job experiences	Learning takes place while the person is on the job doing actual work. Examples include job rotation and job transfers.
Leadership developmental programs	These programs provide targeted, in-depth experiences and classroom-based learning to prepare managers for leadership positions.
Mentoring	A mentor (experienced employee) provides guidance to a mentee (less-experienced employee) with the goal of developing the mentee in her career and personal life.
Coaching	An experienced employee works with a less-experienced employee on a one-on-one basis to develop competencies.
Team-based learning	Individuals learn by working together in teams. There are a variety of teams, such as global teams, virtual teams, problem-solving teams, and special teams (see Chapter 8, "Learning and Development Through Teamwork (Trend 5)," for more information).
Participation in meetings/conferences	Individuals learn by attending or participating in professional conferences and meetings. These conferences/meetings can be in international locations.

Development Practice	Description
Corporate university	This type of entity addresses the learning needs of the organization. It covers various stakeholders of the organization, including employees at all levels, customers, and at times, employees of competitors. Examples include McDonalds' Hamburger University and GE's Crotonville University.[3]
Stretch assignments	These types of assignments/projects push employees beyond their comfort zone, placing them in situations that are different from which they are accustomed; assignments also stretch employees' knowledge, skills, and ability to acquire new competencies.
Action learning	Individuals work in small teams to solve actual problems facing the organization. Each person learns as he tackles the problem with other team members.
Shadowing	An individual learns through observing or *shadowing* another person who is experienced and an expert. Learning occurs through observation and interaction.

As highlighted throughout this book, each activity has to be customized to suit the needs of individual learners. Figure 9.1 lists the attributes for each activity. Each attribute can be visualized on a continuum, and collectively the attributes can be considered a menu of choices for designing development programs or activities. It is important to note that for each attribute, the ends of the continuum are not necessarily opposites but may be complementary.

Learning distance refers to the physical distance between trainers/instructors and learners. Learning delivery formats can be online/virtual (the trainer and trainees are geographically separated), offline/in-person (an individual teaches in person), or a combination of both.

Content delivery refers to how the instructor interacts with the learners and delivers the learning material. The options include synchronous (occurs in real time with the trainer and learners participating at the same time) or asynchronous (the trainer and learners are not present at the same time).

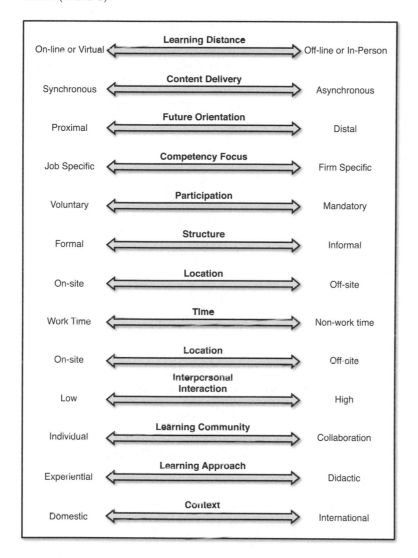

Figure 9.1 Development activity menu[4]

Future orientation refers to the time horizon of the developmental activity, which can develop individuals for jobs that need to be filled in the short term (proximal) or in the long term (distal).

Competency focus describes the type of skills that are being developed. Job-specific skills are those skills necessary to do a specific job, whereas firm-specific skills are general skills that can be applied to multiple jobs.

Participation refers to whether participation in development is voluntary or mandatory.

Structure refers to who controls the learning process. Formal structure is instructor-controlled and led, whereas informal structure is learner-controlled.

Location is where the actual learning takes place. Onsite learning occurs at the company site, whereas offsite learning occurs at locations outside the company.

Time refers to when learning takes place. It can take place during work hours (work time) or take place outside work hours (nonwork times).

Interpersonal interaction is the extent of interaction among learners or between the instructor and the learners (low versus high).

Learning community refers to the extent to which learners cooperate with each other and work together. Learning community can be individualized (one to three people) or collaborative (greater than three people).

Learning approach refers to how learning takes place. It can either be experiential (learning from experience) or didactic (learners passively listen to the instructor).

Context of learning can be domestic (learning takes place in one country) or international (learning takes place in different countries).

What Is Extreme Development?

As indicated in Table 9.1 and Figure 9.1, individuals may be developed in a variety of ways; however, selecting the most appropriate development activities to match the developmental needs of an individual can be challenging for training and development professionals (see Chapter 6, "Customized Learning and Learner Control (Trend 6)," for a discussion on this topic). As mentioned earlier, all development activities are not the same, and it is highly unrealistic to assume that development activities will be the same for all employees in an organization.

There is increasing agreement among management researchers and practitioners that good development takes time and resources, both of which are a luxury that organizations and managers do not always possess. Because most managers are often strapped for time and resources,[5] more has to be done with less.

An important challenge facing managers today is maximizing learning in a short period of time. One approach is to place individuals outside their comfort zones to accelerate learning. This is called *extreme development.* The idea of taking people out of their comfort zones for learning purposes is not new and has been discussed in adventure education[6] and sports research for years. It has, perhaps, acquired some urgency in organizations and especially in management. Extreme development can be traced back to research conducted on job-based learning,[7] which has shown that managerial jobs have certain developmental components such as creating change and managing high levels of responsibility.[8] Jobs with challenging or developmental components offer learning opportunities that contribute significantly to the development of competencies.[9]

Relative to extreme development, the notion of accelerated learning is also not new and goes back about 40 years.[10] Accelerated learning has been examined in leadership development research,[11] as the idea behind it is to complete learning in a shorter period of time compared with traditional learning.[12] This is accomplished by streamlining time frames, acquiring and retaining content faster, and removing/reducing barriers to learning, such as anxiety, stress, a poor attitude toward acquiring new knowledge, and a fear of failure.[13]

Extreme development involves moving beyond one's comfort zone and accelerated learning. Overall, there are certain conditions wherein extreme development would add much value to an organization and to an individual:

- **Extreme development has to be customized:** It is not for everyone. Each person's comfort zone is unique.[14] It is important to identify those individuals who would be well suited for extreme development, as no one should feel overburdened or overwhelmed by a developmental challenge.[15] For example, individuals with stronger learning goal orientation can benefit from extreme development because learning goal orientation can accelerate development.[16]

- **Extreme development is a continuous process:** Similar to what athletes experience in training and workouts, no variety in thought or approach can lead to a plateau. In general, a person can eventually become so accustomed to something "new" that the novelty of it wears off and the person begins to feel comfortable in his once "new" routine.[17] Hence, this does not leave much room for growth. This is why it is always important for individuals to keep challenging themselves to move out of their comfort zones.

- **Individuals need prior knowledge:** Applying the cognitive perspective to learning is useful here (see Chapter 2, "Adult Learning and Development"). Individuals need prior related knowledge to assimilate and use new knowledge. Learning can be accelerated when new knowledge is related to the individual's existing knowledge base.

Extreme development can be used to develop employees at all levels. Every development activity listed in Table 9.1 can have an element of discomfort ranging from low to extreme. Stretch assignments are an example of an extreme development activity.

The Importance of Stretch Assignments

Stretch assignments are becoming more essential for developing high-potential employees for future leadership roles. They refer to projects or jobs that have significant developmental or learning components, such as managing uncertainty and change, influencing others, and building coalitions. Stretch assignments take individuals out of their comfort zones and are different from previous jobs and experiences.[18] Moreover, the individual is motivated by the challenge and the goal of learning new competencies.

Certain design issues must be addressed to ensure that learning occurs in the context of a stretch assignment:[19]

- A continuous learning culture can promote and accelerate learning by encouraging and motivating individuals to participate in "stretch" activities.
- A thorough needs assessment is required to determine specific learning needs. However, learning should build on individuals' willingness to increase their self-confidence and motivation to learn.
- Assignments should be challenging but not to the point where the individual is overwhelmed and risks failing.
- Ongoing and formal feedback, especially from a mentor or a coach, is critical for improving learning.

Development practices like stretch assignments assume that learners are predisposed to acquiring competencies from challenging experiences. One type of ability that is important for learning is learning agility.[20]

The Importance of Learning Agility

The concept of learning agility is rooted in leadership development literature as a predictor of leadership potential.[21] However, despite its prevalence and importance, there is no consensus on the precise definition of learning agility. Some have defined it in terms of the ability to learn from experiences and using those experiences to improve performance.[22] Others have defined it in terms of a mindset and a corresponding set of practices associated with the development of that mindset.[23] Most recently, it was defined in terms of speed and flexibility.[24] A common theme among these definitions is that learning from experience is a fundamental part of development.

In brief, the argument is that when compared with unsuccessful executives, or what the literature refers to as *derailed executives,* successful executives are more likely to have distinct and diverse experiences throughout their careers. Further, individual differences play an important role in learning from experience. Essentially, attitudes toward learning and motivation to learn from past experiences differentiate executives who are successful from those who are not.[25]

For these reasons, learning agility is becoming increasingly popular and has stimulated considerable research interest and activity among academics and human resource management professionals in recent years. Some findings assert

- Learning agility is not related to age, ethnicity, or gender.[26]
- Learning agility is increasingly used as a tool to identify high potentials[27] and leadership talent.[28]

- Learning agility is related to career success. It is a strong indicator of increased upward mobility and higher compensation.[29]
- Learning agility has a normal distribution among the general employed population.[30]
- Learning agility enables individuals to determine what no longer works and find new ways to manage new, unique, and different challenges.[31]

Given the importance of learning agility, organizations will continue to attract and develop individuals with learning agility for several reasons:

- Executive and managerial jobs are becoming more complex, increasingly unstructured, ambiguous, knowledge-intensive, and require more than one set of competencies.
- Most development occurs on the job in the context of work experiences. The ability to continuously learn from experiences and apply acquired knowledge from experiences is an essential competency.
- With a clear shortage of talent in global labor markets and increases in the time it takes to attract and select talent from outside the organization, it is easier to identify talent from within the organization.

It is important to remember that a major assumption of learning agility is that individual differences play an important role in learning from experience. Some of the individual-level characteristics that are related to learning agility include learning goal orientation, cognitive ability, openness to experience, and self-awareness.

Learning agility can be viewed as an ability to *adapt quickly* to new learning situations and contexts (for example, challenging experiences or job assignments) to maximize learning.[32] Examples of adapting include

- Determine the right combination of attitude, skills, and knowledge that is needed to learn from challenging experiences. Agile learners ask the question, "What do I need to know to learn from this experience?"

- Find ways of overcoming barriers to learning. Agile learners ask the question, "What will prevent me from learning from this experience?"

- Seek opportunities to apply the new competencies. Agile learners ask the question, "How can I use what I have learned?"

In the near future, the concept of learning agility will need to evolve to be more inclusive of the changing nature of work and the changing nature of the global economy (see Chapter 1, "Forces Shaping the Corporate Learning Function"). Only those individuals who are truly committed to learning quickly from experiences that are ambiguous, unique, and challenging will succeed in the turbulent business environment that lies ahead.

Summary

This chapter focused on extreme development and on two important aspects of extreme development: stretch assignments and learning agility. The chapter began by describing what development is and the various types of developmental practices. The chapter then discussed the concept of extreme development in terms of taking people out of their comfort zones for learning purposes. This chapter also discussed the importance of stretch assignments and how a continuous learning culture provides a context for stretch assignments. The chapter closed with a discussion on learning agility.

10 —————————————————————————————

The New Experts (Trend 7)

What's in this chapter:

- What is expertise?
- Developing expertise
- Experts and reverse knowledge transfer

Individuals, no matter the type of organization for which they work or the work they do, can and do confront the need to specialize. The extent of specialization varies according to a number of factors, chief among them labor market dynamics. As organizations become flatter and jobs become more complex, individuals in various professions need to gain *expertise* to be successful. However, as discussed in Chapters 1–3, there are strong pressures changing how we learn and develop; this, subsequently, has an impact on how we develop expertise in the context of changes taking place in today's business environment.

This chapter discusses the seventh and the final trend: the new experts.

What Is Expertise?

It is easy to look for experts or try to locate an expert when we need one. We all need experts, whether it is at home or in business; experts can exist at different levels of management. Experts are becoming more common in organizations, as they provide a valuable resource to any manager or supervisor.

Expertise refers to advanced or in-depth competencies (for example, knowledge, skills, and abilities) in a specific area, also known as domain-specific competencies.[1] These areas are usually narrow and extensively focused, such as interventional cardiology, securities law, and actuarial analyses.

Although each expert has unique traits, experiences, and competencies, there are certain commonalities that can be found among experts. Their level of expertise

- Should lead to improved performance that is reliable and superior to that of nonexperts[2]
- Should lead to concrete results or successful outcomes[3]
- Can be replicated by others[4]

In addition, experts differ from novices in a number of ways. Their ability to see patterns in information and their ability to filter relevant information from irrelevant information[5] are among the things that distinguish them from novices. They have more knowledge about their content area and recognize patterns, specifically how different concepts are connected.[6]

An important question, then, is how is expertise developed?

Developing Expertise

One point is certain: Developing expertise takes time. Individuals go through various stages of learning before becoming an expert. One of the most popular models relevant to developing expertise is the five-stage Dreyfus model:[7]

- **Stage 1—Novice:** In this stage, the individual is considered a beginner who follows strict guidelines or logical rules to guide his actions and behaviors. The beginner pays less attention to the context or environment in which situations take place (for example, less situational perception).

- **Stage 2—Advanced Beginner:** The individual recognizes that context is important and enters the Advanced Beginner stage. In this stage, the person begins to engage in completing tasks or assignments independently and gains experience (creates prior knowledge). She starts noticing important environmental elements but still does not have a complete understanding of the environment.

- **Stage 3—Competent:** At this stage, the individual conceptually understands the situation and the environment. He gains more experience and starts coping with information overload and problem solving. There is a need to set priorities, make plans, and develop routines. The individual understands that priorities and planning may change with the circumstances.

- **Stage 4—Proficient:** In this stage, the individual can see the complete situation or the big picture. The person begins to understand what is important in any particular situation, how situations vary, and how there are similarities and differences for each given situation. The individual engages in more analyses and decision making and develops a thorough understanding of rules, guidelines, and theories.

- **Stage 5—Expert:** At this stage, the individual becomes an expert. She uses intuition to understand situations. Rules or guidelines no longer become the sole baseline for making decisions. The person has a deep understanding of how concepts are connected to one another. Based on past experience, the expert sees what needs to be achieved and how to achieve it. Essentially, the expert envisions the possibilities that exist.

Time and experiences are considered important elements in developing expertise.[8] But there are specific practices, attitudes, and behaviors that can lead to expertise:

- **Practice is critical:** The concept of deliberate practice[9] has been extensively used to emphasize how an individual can improve current skills and/or acquire new competencies through practice.[10]

- **Experts develop other experts:** Most experts, at some point in their learning process, have been guided by individuals, coaches, and mentors who are also experts.[11]

- **Learning is continuous:**[12] Experts realize that learning does not end. They continue to put effort and time into maintaining what they know; they also learn new competencies.[13]

- **There is a strong willingness to learn:** Experts are willing to participate in learning activities and experiences; they have a high motivation to learn.[14]

- **Thinking strategically is important:**[15] Experts employ their strategic thinking skills to plan and set goals. While setting goals, they know how to achieve them.[16]

- **Learning agility is important:** Learning agility can facilitate developing expertise. (See Chapter 9, "Extreme Development: Stretch Assignments and Learning Agility (Trend 6).")

An interesting question is, has the process or outcome of developing expertise evolved or changed?

The outcome has not changed. Experts are still defined by the specialized competencies they develop. However, the process for developing expertise is changing for several reasons:

- **Technology is an accelerator:** In industries or professions that require creativity, innovation, and entrepreneurship, or professions that require in-depth, domain-specific knowledge, experts are most likely to stay ahead of computers and technology.[17] Technology is not likely to replace experts, but the technologies available today (discussed in Chapter 4, "Technology-Based Learning (Trend 1)") can accelerate the development of expertise.

- **Knowledge needs to be sliced:** Experts in a variety of fields, especially in scientific fields, possess significant specialized knowledge. Overall, they know more today than in the past. As a result, experts have to specialize further so that they will not become overwhelmed or get distracted with existing knowledge in a particular area.

- **Own the expertise:** Experts have to become entrepreneurs and transform their expertise into a business model to survive intellectually. This is especially true because knowledge has an expiration date. Experts can lose their competitive advantage in the labor market if expertise is not managed properly.

Essential Expertise

There is also another type of expertise that I call *essential expertise*. Every manager needs it. Essential expertise refers to a set of core competencies that must be mastered to survive in highly competitive labor markets. Competencies include

- Critical thinking and problem solving[18] (decision-making ability)
- Effective communication[19] (written and oral skills)
- Collaboration and team building[20] (working with a diverse group of people)

- Creativity and innovation skills[21] (creating something new)
- Strategic imagination[22] (visualizing future opportunities and possibilities)
- Provocative inquiry[23] (asking critical and intelligent questions)
- Cultural agility[24] (working and living successfully in cross-cultural situations)

Experts and Reverse Knowledge Transfer

From a learning perspective, organizations can consider using their subject matter experts as trainers, instructors, or facilitators during budget cuts or when there is a need to design specialized programs.[25]

There are three important benefits to preparing and utilizing subject matter experts as instructors:[26]

- **Reputation:** Subject matter experts are considered experts in their respective fields and this can enhance their reputation as instructors.
- **Company-specific knowledge:** Subject matter experts have internal knowledge about their organizations, specifically about the organization's culture, strategy, and practices. This adds to the credibility of these experts.
- **Career development:** The opportunity to train can provide subject matter experts with a new career path and may increase their motivation and commitment to the organization.

When working with subject matter experts, it is important to keep instructional content as simple as possible so that the expert can customize it or develop it further.[27]

It is also possible to utilize subject matter experts as instructional designers if the opportunity to teach or train is not available. Subject matter experts can develop instructional content, design delivery methods, and provide support to other trainers.[28] It is important that subject matter experts and trainers develop a good working relationship by communicating on a regular basis.[29] Further, it is beneficial for organizations to encourage collaboration between designers and experts.

Summary

This chapter presented the topic of "expertise" in terms of new experts. The chapter described what expertise is and how experts differ from novices. It addressed an important question of how expertise is developed. More specifically, the chapter described the various stages of learning that individuals go through before becoming experts. The chapter then discussed specific practices, attitudes, and behaviors that can lead to expertise. Following this, the chapter discussed the notion of "essential expertise," which refers to a set of core competencies that must be mastered by every manager to survive in highly competitive labor markets. Finally, the chapter closed with a brief discussion of the role of knowledge transfer in the context of expertise.

Part III

Strategic Directions for Training and Development

11

Investment in Workforce Learning and Development

What's in this chapter:

- The investment perspective: corporate learning strategy
- The investment perspective: a dedicated talent management function
- Evaluation of investments in workforce learning and development

As mentioned in the first chapter, it has become imperative for organizations to depend on the learning function to develop a workforce that has the competencies needed to be successful in a global economy. Organizations that view workforce development as an investment rather than a cost are more likely to be successful in the long run. These organizations take an "investment perspective" and focus on the benefits that result from development.

This chapter attempts to describe the investment perspective and discusses how to evaluate the benefits that result from investments in workforce learning and development.

The Investment Perspective: Corporate Learning Strategy

The investment perspective involves viewing the learning function (see Chapter 1, "Forces Shaping the Corporate Learning Function") as a strategic partner and providing the necessary support to this function to increase its value in the organization.

The investment perspective requires

- Developing a learning strategy
- Investing in training and development practices

Developing a Corporate Learning Strategy

Before discussing a corporate learning strategy, it is important to understand strategic management and business strategy.

Strategic management, in broad terms, is a process that includes planning, decisions, and moves that managers use to operate an organization to support its goals and objectives.[1] This process includes various types of business strategies that provide management with a guideline or an action plan to manage different types of resources (such as human resource, financial, and technology) for developing sustainable competitive advantage.[2]

Business strategies can be developed proactively or reactively.[3] A proactive approach to strategy development involves anticipating future trends and developing a business strategy to manage future threats, challenges, and opportunities in the marketplace. In contrast, a reactive approach to strategy development involves reacting to the threats, challenges, and opportunities that the organization is experiencing in the marketplace.

There are different types of business strategies. Some occur at the organizational level (for example, how a company grows or diversifies), and some occur at the business unit level (such as how each business unit of the organization operates). From an HR perspective, three business unit strategies[4] are considered relevant:

- Cost leadership strategy
- Differentiation business strategy
- Focus strategy

An organization that uses cost leadership strategy competes on the basis of keeping costs lower than its competitors. A firm that pursues a differentiation strategy produces products and services that are uniquely different from the products and services of competitors. Finally, an organization that utilizes the focus strategy concentrates on a small or niche market or segment and either competes on the basis of lower costs or product differentiation.

The role of HR is to develop practices and policies that support the organization's business strategies. HR practices and policies vary with the type of business strategy. For example, an organization using a cost leadership strategy will develop training programs for employees who work part time. Companies that focus on the differentiation business strategy will develop training and development programs that focus on employees who are creative and innovative.

So where do the corporate learning strategies fit in?

A *corporate learning strategy* refers to the combination of policies and practices (also referred to as activities in this book) that are used to provide competencies that are needed by the organization's workforce. The goal of the corporate learning strategy is to support the organization's business strategy.[5]

An important question is, How do you develop corporate learning strategies? One approach is to design learning strategies based on the various employee groups that exist within the organization. This approach is based on the notion of workforce differentiation or segmentation.[6] This approach is popular in the field of talent management and suggests that employees who add more value to the organization should be treated differently. Employees can be categorized as *A, B,* and *C* players, with *A* players being their most valuable and talented.

In addition to categorizing employees, jobs can be grouped into *A* positions, *B* positions, and *C* positions based on how critical a job is to the organization's success. The idea is to have *A* players in *A* positions and *B* Players in *B* positions.[7]

Each employee group can have a unique learning strategy or strategies. For example, *A* players will probably receive the most extensive and valuable learning practices, such as leadership development programs and stretch assignments.

Another approach is to develop learning strategies based on the level of management: upper management, middle management, and lower management. Similar to *A* players, the upper-level management can receive the costly and extensive type of learning practices.

The Investment Perspective: A Dedicated Talent Management Function

As mentioned in Chapter 1, the investment perspective suggests that the learning function should be part of a talent management function. *Talent management* refers to an approach that organizations use to attract, develop, retain, and mobilize employees who are most valuable and important to their strategic success, both domestically and internationally.

The learning function and its corporate learning strategy should support the other areas of talent management. Figure 11.1 shows the relationship between the learning function and other talent management areas.

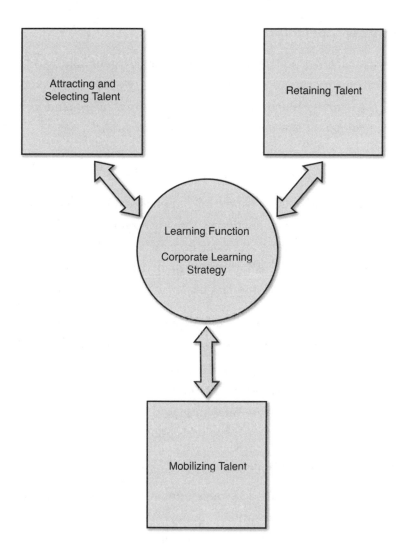

Figure 11.1 Alignments between the learning function and other talent management areas

As Figure 11.1 shows, the learning function is at the center of talent management. It supports the three other areas of talent management, but the relationship is mutually beneficial. The learning function also receives support from other areas of talent management.

Attracting and Selecting Talent

This area includes policies and practices that are generally associated with recruitment and selection. There are two important concerns for the learning function: *learning function and talent planning* and *learning function and developing an employer brand.*[8]

Learning Function and Talent Planning

This involves anticipating future talent needs in terms of the type of competencies that will be needed by the organization in the future. An important concern here is attracting talent when the labor markets are tight, meaning there is a shortage of talent. The role of the learning function is to support talent planning by

- Developing existing employees in case organizations cannot attract the appropriate talent from the labor markets

- Training or developing "raw talent"—those individuals available in the labor market who do not have the required competencies, but have the potential for growth

Learning Function and Developing an Employer Brand

Here, the concern is to develop a human resource reputation[9] to attract talent. Human resource reputation is the perception or impression people outside the organization have about the organization's image as an employer.

By investing in the learning function

- Organizations send signals to various stakeholders, including potential applicants, that the employees and their career development/growth are important. This can improve an organization's employer brand.

- Organizations can attract internal talent (people who already work for the company) and eventually prevent them from leaving the organization.

Overall, organizations can effectively use the learning function to attract applicants from the labor markets and people who already work for the organization.

Retaining Talent

This area focuses on policies and practices that prevent talented employees from leaving the organization. There are two important concerns for the learning function: *learning function and employee retention* and *learning function and loss of talent.*[10]

Learning Function and Employee Retention

As discussed in Chapter 1, an important challenge for organizations is to retain talent in the context of a "low employee commitment world." The reality is that talented employees are always in the job search mode, even when they are working and satisfied with their current jobs. The organization has a short window of opportunity with the talented employee. From the organization's perspective, the goal is to extract the maximum value from the employee in the shortest period of time.[11] The goal of the learning function here is to

- Accelerate development of talented employees.
- Extract knowledge from talented employees before they leave the organization.

Learning Function and Loss of Talent

A players can't last forever. Their career paths or career progressions have to be monitored carefully. To what extent and for how long can employees sustain their talents to remain in the organization's talent pool?[12] What practices are in place to halt the slide of talent? There are a variety of reasons for the decline of *A* players, such as lack of motivation and skill obsolescence.[13] The role of the learning function is central here, especially in preventing skill obsolescence.

Mobilizing Talent

This area is mostly relevant to international organizations and includes policies and practices that move employees across regions or countries. There are two key concerns for the learning function: *learning function and global mobility* and *learning function and managing Adult Third Culture Kids*.[14]

Learning Function and Global Mobility

There are three groups of employees that a multinational organization moves to various countries and locations. Before describing these employee groups, it is important to understand how a multinational organization is structured.

Multinational organizations conduct business outside their countries of origin with revenue coming from a variety of countries and locations. A multinational organization usually has headquarters in the home country or the country of origin and has subsidiaries in different regions and countries.

Multinational organizations use three types of employee groups to staff subsidiaries in foreign countries. These employees include

- Parent country nationals (PCNs)
- Third country nationals (TCNs)
- Host country nationals (HCNs)

PCNs are defined as citizens of the country where the corporate headquarters is located. TCNs refer to individuals who are neither citizens of the country where the multinational organization is headquartered nor citizens of the country where the foreign subsidiary is located. Finally, HCNs are citizens of the country where the subsidiary is located.

It is important to note that both PCNs and TCNs are expatriates who leave their home countries to work in foreign countries. Most of the time, these two groups are selected from a pool that is highly talented. Their success becomes paramount to the success of the multinational organization.

An important role of the learning function is to prepare PCNs and TCNs to successfully live and work in foreign countries. Three training practices that are normally used to prepare PCNs and TCNs include cross-cultural training, diversity training, and language training.[15]

Cross-cultural training is designed to help individuals adjust to living and working conditions in the new country. Diversity training is more narrowly focused and is designed to help employees effectively work with a diverse workforce. Foreign language training focuses on providing language skills to successfully communicate with people from a variety of countries.[16]

Out of the three practices, cross-cultural training is considered an essential practice to develop high-potential talent. To be effective, cross-cultural training has to be customized to the needs of the expatriate. Expatriates can be categorized into four types:[17]

- Technical
- Functional/tactical
- Developmental/high potential
- Strategic/executive

The technical assignment requires only minimal interaction with host nationals and is in an organizational setting fairly typical to the setting of the home country. The functional assignment is similar to the technical assignment with one distinct difference—significant interactions with host nationals are necessary for the assignment to be deemed successful. Expatriates on developmental assignments are usually sent for a short period of time (about 6 to 12 months) to gain some international exposure and experience. High-profile employees (such as general managers and vice presidents) who are being groomed to move into higher levels of management in the near future usually fill the strategic assignments.

The preceding categorization of expatriates suggests that competencies required to be successful in foreign countries can vary depending on the type of assignment. Training practices for expatriates can be visualized on a continuum ranging from practical information training (knowledge about a country) to intercultural effectiveness skills training (awareness of appropriate norms and behaviors in the host country).[18] Thus, training for people sent on a technical assignment, which does not require significant interactions with the host nationals, needs to be centered around providing practical information training (for example, information on the shopping and transportation systems of the host country). Training methods like audiovisuals and self-learning videos may provide the required level of training. In contrast, the training of people sent on developmental/high potential assignments and strategic/executive assignments, which both require significant interactions with host nationals for successful completion of assignments, must focus more on intercultural effectiveness skills training. One training session may be provided prior to departure, and several sessions must be conducted at different times after the assignee has been placed in the host country for at least one month.[19] Training techniques such as simulation games and behavior modeling may be appropriate in this situation.[20] However, functional/tactical assignees who are sent to fill technical positions but who interact with host nationals on a daily basis may need training that extends beyond practical information training, but that is not as extensive as the intercultural effectiveness skills training.

In addition to practical information training, training types such as area studies training (knowledge involving political, economic, and cultural facts about the host country) and cultural awareness training (knowledge about the host culture) through training techniques such as culture assimilators may be appropriate.

Learning Function and Managing Adult Third Culture Kids

One group of individuals that is extremely useful to multinational organizations is Adult Third Culture Kids (ATCKs). ATCKs are individuals who have spent significant periods of childhood living outside their parents' culture(s).[21] They acquire extensive early international experiences by living in multiple countries, speaking multiple languages, and at times growing up in diverse or multicultural families. They have what is referred to as the "global mindset"[22]—these individuals are future expatriates and are ready to move from country to country without much cross-cultural training. More important, they have the potential to develop and move into global leadership positions. The role of the learning function here is to use accelerated leadership development programs or stretch assignments to develop ATCKs for global leadership positions.

Evaluation of Investments in Workforce Learning and Development

The ultimate goal of any learning activity, whether it is training or development, is to bring about a change in learning and in performance on the job. Evaluation of investments in workforce development (EIWD) refers to the process of determining the effectiveness of corporate learning at three levels:

- **EIWD at the business unit or function level:** Evaluating the effectiveness of the learning function

- **EIWD at the systems or practice level:** Evaluating the effectiveness of the training or development activity
- **EIWD at the individual level:** Evaluating the effectiveness of the learner

Evaluating the Effectiveness of the Learning Function

Here, the focus is on determining how effective the learning function is in meeting its goals and objectives. There are several important outcomes of the learning function and how it affects the following:

- **The overall corporate learning strategy:** How effective is the learning function in formulating and implementing a corporate learning strategy?
- **Culture of continuous learning:** How effective is the learning function in developing and maintaining a culture of continuous learning in the organization as a whole, and in various business units (for example, marketing, finance, and accounting)?
- **Technology-based learning:** How effective is the learning function in utilizing the most current technology-based learning (such as m-learning)?
- **Business goals:** How effective is the learning function in supporting the overall vision, values, and strategy of the organization?
- **HR goals:** How effective is the learning function in supporting the goals and objectives of the HR function?
- **Talent attraction/selection:** How effective is the learning function in supporting the goals and objectives of the talent acquisition systems (attracting and selecting talent)?
- **Talent retention:** How effective is the learning function in supporting the goals and objectives of the talent retention systems (for example, reducing turnover and retaining talent)?

- **Talent mobility:** How effective is the learning function in supporting the goals and objectives of the talent mobility systems such as, moving employees across countries and regions)?

In addition to these outcomes, several metrics can be used to examine the strength of human capital that exists within the learning function:

- Number of full-time employees (measures the size of the function)

- Number of part-time employees (measures the size of the function)

- Number of full-time or part-time employees with professional degrees, certifications, or training (such as, Ph.D., MBA, MSc, and other industry-related certifications) (measures the talent in the function)

- Number of full-time trainers and/or instructors (measures the flexibility of the function)

- Number of part-time trainers and instructors (measures the flexibility of the function)

Evaluating the Effectiveness of the Training or Development Activities and Programs

Here, the goal is to examine each of the learning activities or practices and designs of the various learning programs to make sure that they are working properly. This is sometimes referred to as *formative evaluation*.[23]

Some of the important areas of investigation include

- Are the training and development programs creating the best possible learning experience?

- Are there any new learning technologies that can improve the training and development programs and make them (programs) more effective?

- Can the training and development programs be customized to suit the specific needs of the learners?

- Do the training and development programs engage learners to increase knowledge acquisition and retention?

- Do the training and development programs have the right blend of informal learning, formal learning, mobile learning, and social learning?

Most of the time, the data to conduct a formative evaluation comes from[24]

- Learners or customers

- Trainers or instructors

- Subject matter experts

- Managers

- Instructional designers

Evaluating the Effectiveness of the Learner

Out of the three types of EIWDs, determining if learners have acquired the learning material, and if they can use and apply the new competencies, is considered the most important aspect of evaluation. The main point is that if learners don't learn, the whole learning function can fall apart. Good learning is visible to others. There are various methods to evaluate the change that occurs in learners after participating in a learning activity,[25] and a general consensus is that the best outcome of learning is conceptualized as multidimensional.[26]

The most popular approach to learning evaluation has been Kirkpatrick's four levels of evaluation.[27] This approach suggests that training and developmental activities can be evaluated according to four criteria or levels—reaction, learning, behavior, and results:

- **Level 1—Reaction:** Evaluation at this level focuses on what the participants or learners thought of a particular training or developmental activity. (For example, were they satisfied with the training?)

- **Level 2—Learning:** Evaluation at this level concentrates on the extent to which individuals or participants learned or improved competencies (such as knowledge, skills, abilities) during or by the end of the training or developmental activity.

- **Level 3—Behavior:** Evaluation at this level refers to the change(s) or improvements in job-related behaviors due to the training or developmental activity.

- **Level 4—Results:** Evaluation at this level looks at organizational performance in terms of increased production, decreased costs, and increased profits.

In general, Kirkpatrick's levels 1 and 2 can be measured either during or immediately after the training or developmental activity, and Kirkpatrick's levels 3 and 4 can be measured after individuals have completed the training or developmental activity.

Level 3 is also known as *transfer of learning*, which is the extent to which an individual can *generalize* and *maintain* the learning that occurred during the training or development program. *Generalization* refers to an ability to apply the acquired competencies to work and nonwork problems and situations that are similar but not identical to problems and situations encountered in the training or development program. *Maintenance* refers to an individual's ability to continuously maintain and use the acquired competencies over time.[28] Hence, transfer of learning is an important indicator of learning.

In addition to Kirkpatrick's four levels of evaluation, there is another popular approach that focuses on three types of learning outcomes:[29]

- **Cognitive learning outcomes:** These include the acquisition of different types of knowledge (see Chapter 3, "The Art of Knowledge Acquisition"), including higher-level knowledge.

- **Skill-based learning outcomes:** These include technical and or motor skills.

- **Affective learning outcomes:** These include learner's attitudes, motivation, and goals.

Finally, more recently, there has been considerable discussion around calculating the return on investments (ROI) of learning, which, in general terms, uses a cost-benefit analysis that examines the costs and benefits of a learning activity.[30]

It should be noted that regardless of which approach is used to evaluate learning, some fundamental principles of evaluation need to be understood:

- **Understand the process through which learning from the individual impacts job performance and organizational performance:** In general, learning that results from participating in a learning activity (training or development) does not lead directly to change in job performance, let alone organizational performance. Rather, learning—whether it is in the form of knowledge, skills, or ability—influences intermediate outcomes, such as behaviors that lead to changes in job performance. This is a sequential process that takes time and does not happen instantly.

  In addition, the jump from individual learning to organizational performance is huge. There are many intervening variables between individual learning and organizational outcomes, such as revenue, costs, profits, and so on. It is possible that a learning activity was successful in increasing knowledge, but the subsequent impact of knowledge on job performance or organizational performance depends on factors like organizational culture, support from employees and managers, and so on.

- **Understand the differences between correlation and causality. Correlation does not imply causation:** Correlation refers to the statistical relationship between two variables in terms of how one variable varies with the other (how one variable changes when the other changes). For example, the number of hours of training per year per employee is positively correlated with job performance. However, this does not mean that the number of hours of training per year per employee *caused* the change in job performance. Causation occurs when one variable causes a change in another variable. One way to determine causality is to use rigorous experimental designs.[31]

Summary

This chapter addressed the important topic of investing in workforce learning and development in terms of two perspectives: the corporate learning strategy perspective and a talent management perspective. The corporate learning perspective focuses on developing a learning strategy and investing in training and development practices. In contrast, the talent management perspective focuses on integrating the leaning function with the talent management function. The chapter then focused on evaluation of investments in workforce learning and development at three different levels: learning function, training and development activities, and the learner.

12

The Future of Training and Development

What's in this chapter:

- Future of leadership and managerial competencies
- Future of forces shaping the corporate learning function
- Future of adult learning and development
- Future of knowledge acquisition
- Future of technology-based learning
- Future of informal learning
- Future of customized learning and learner control
- Future of continuous learning
- Future of learning and development through teamwork
- Future of extreme development
- Future of the new experts
- Future of investments in workforce learning and development

A plethora of reports, studies, and research demonstrates that there are important trends reshaping workplace training and development. The ideas and concepts presented in this book capture the emerging trends that will continue to evolve in the future. One thing is certain: Significant changes have occurred in the past decade with regard to how organizations are managing the learning function.

Descriptions of several themes that highlight some of the changes that will probably occur in the future are the focus of this chapter.

Future of Leadership and Managerial Competencies

As discussed in Chapter 1, "Forces Shaping the Corporate Learning Function," jobs and work are evolving at an increasingly rapid pace. Keeping pace with the demand for jobs and work is an increasing demand for talented people. Managerial and leadership competencies are changing to accommodate these developments.

Considerable research has been done to identify the competencies future leaders and managers will need. In their study, "Future Work Skills 2020" (p. 8–12),[1] the Institute for the Future and the University of Phoenix Research Institute identified ten core competencies: *sense-making, social intelligence, novel and adaptive thinking, cross-cultural competency, computational thinking, new-media literacy, transdisciplinarity, design mindset, cognitive load management,* and *virtual collaboration.*

Similarly, in the study "21st Century Skills and the Workplace" (p.7–10), which was conducted by Gallup, in collaboration with Microsoft Partners in Learning and the Pearson Foundation, researchers developed a twenty-first century skills index focusing on seven areas:[2] *technology, knowledge construction, skilled communication, real-world problem solving, self-regulation, collaboration,* and *global awareness.*

Further, scholars and professionals (Richard Florida, Mark Penn, Malcolm Gladwell, Wendell Williams, and Gary Marsh) have also attempted to identify future competencies, such as *creativity* and *entrepreneurial spirit,*[3] *ability to lead diverse teams* (members with different personality types),[4] *idea discovery* (finding new ideas),[5] *understanding and managing diversity,*[6] *adaptability,*[7] *emotional intelligence,*[8] *strong team skills,*[9] *personal responsibility,*[10] *personal productivity,*[11] *handling difficult situations,*[12] *learning and problem solving,*[13] *planning and organizing,*[14] *interpersonal skills,*[15] and *attitudes, interests, and motivations.*[16]

When examined carefully, these competencies have some common themes:

- **Team-based competencies:**[17] These include effectively working in teams—especially virtual teams—leading a team, managing conflicts in teams, and so forth.

- **Information/knowledge-based competencies:**[18] These include searching for information, discerning fact from fiction, managing information overload, applying information, and so forth.

- **Interaction-based competencies:**[19] These include interacting with people from a variety of backgrounds, interacting virtually, building trust through interactions, distinguishing between useful and worthless interactions, and so forth.

- **Technology-based competencies:**[20] These include awareness and knowledge of new and emerging technologies, learning to use new technologies, unlearning old technologies, and so forth.

- **Career-based competencies:** These include awareness of strengths and weaknesses, setting goals, career planning, seeking new opportunities, and so forth.

- **Cross-culture-based competencies:** These include awareness of cultural differences, fluency in a foreign language(s), working with people from different cultures or countries, using appropriate cultural behaviors, and so forth.

- **Intraculture-based competencies:** These include understanding and appreciating people of different age, ethnic, and religious backgrounds;[21] awareness of group-based differences among people; reducing or decreasing negative stereotyping and prejudice;[22] and so forth.

It is beneficial to note that these competencies have been important and required by many jobs in the past, but they are essential now and will be even more critical in the future, particularly in the industries affected by the changes discussed in Chapter 1.

Future of Forces Shaping the Corporate Learning Function

Chapter 1 examined the major forces that are shaping the corporate learning function. One conclusion that can be reached from the chapter is given that our economic, business, and workplace environments are always changing, new factors or forces will continue to develop in the near future and will affect how organizations manage the learning function. Future themes may include

- **The need for cross-cultural competencies will become critical in most leadership and managerial positions:** Most leadership and managerial jobs in the future may include elements of global work. For example, we now see the emergence of virtual expatriates defined as individuals who do not travel overseas but still work with individuals in different countries through e-mail or virtual technology.

- **The concept of megacities will become popular:** Organizations will pay more attention to megacities with respect to countries. In fact, this is happening now. In addition, megacities will aggressively compete with one another to attract resources and investments, including talent.

- **Talent shortages will become a growing concern for most businesses:** However, at some point in the future, persistent talent shortages will be considered normal. The question is not whether we will have talent shortages, but how voluminous the talent shortages will be in the future. Most organizations will realize that specialists are needed to manage talent. In addition, there is an important debate within human resources management as to whether talent management will have more significance than human resources management. It will be interesting to see the outcome of this debate because this issue has direct implications for the learning function. A large part of talent management focuses on learning and development of key employees. *The talent management function is part of HR management, which is where talent management should remain.*

- **Workforce segmentation will continue to grow:** The idea that the workforce has to be segmented into categories to be managed efficiently is becoming popular. The concept of workforce segmentation will evolve and develop not only in the United States, but also in the rest of the world. However, widespread segmentation will take time.

  In addition, in the future we are most likely to see bimodal distribution in terms of the different generations at work. On one end of the spectrum, there will be younger workers, relatively speaking, and on the other end, there will be an aging workforce. Managing these two groups of employees will be challenging for most organizations.

- **The nature of careers and jobs will continue to change:** This is an extremely important area and an area that has had significant impact on how people are managed, but more important, on how they are trained and developed. The idea of hybrid careers and fluid jobs will evolve and eventually become permanent. Moreover, this trend will be more prominent in some industries than others, but overall one point is clear: Employee commitment will continue to decline. Individuals are more likely to take control of their careers and become opportunistic workers who are always seeking the next best opportunity, even while employed.

Further, full-time jobs will continue to decline and the notion of an "extended workforce"[23] will become popular. This refers to contingent workers, part-time workers, contractors, and workers in the cloud.[24] The extended workforce will be managed and developed like the full-time workforce.[25]

Future of Adult Learning and Development

Chapter 2, "Adult Learning and Development," discussed topics related to how adults learn, specifically describing theories and concepts that are relevant today. There are two themes that will have a major impact in the future:

- **Importance of cognitivism and constructivism:** As described in Chapter 2, three important perspectives are widely used to explain how learning occurs in adults: cognitivism, behaviorism, and constructivism. An important question to be raised is whether these perspectives will continue to explain learning in the future. Despite the changes that are taking place now, the fundamentals of how adults learn still hold true and will remain unchanged in the future. However, cognitivism and constructivism will grow in popularity because of the issues discussed in Chapters 5, 6, and 7.

- **Future of fragmented learning:** The concept of fragmented learning is interesting and has the potential to be developed further. Fragmented learning will not become another learning theory, but it is an approach HR professionals can use to enhance learning. However, in the future information will be imparted in a fragmented way; the person who can integrate all concepts in a timely and efficient manner will be described as a successful learner.

Future of Knowledge Acquisition

Chapter 3, "The Art of Knowledge Acquisition," examined the idea of knowledge acquisition at the individual level. It described the knowledge economy and the knowledge workforce. The chapter also examined, in detail, different types of knowledge and the interplay between tacit knowledge and specific knowledge. Some of the themes that may emerge in the future include

- **Significance of tacit and specific knowledge:** It is clear that knowledge and competitive advantage are related, but all types of knowledge are not equal; competitive advantage will continue to depend on how tacit and specific knowledge is.

- **Seriousness of information overload:** Chapter 3 discussed the concepts of knowledge search and information overload. These two concepts will play an important role in how HR/training and development professionals design learning activities and how individuals learn. Information overload will be a serious concern and may eventually negatively impact an individual's ability to filter out irrelevant information; this will reduce the quality of learning.

  In addition, individuals will develop sophisticated filters to differentiate between/among different types of information and knowledge.[26] Individuals with strong filters may have an advantage over others.

- **Importance of knowledge transfer:** The topic of knowledge transfer will continue to be an important issue for the next several years. Knowledge transfer is likely to become extremely useful in the future as organizations develop processes to capture tacit knowledge from people who leave their organizations (younger workers changing jobs or older workers retiring). In addition, succession planning, which refers to the process of developing current talent for future roles, will be defined in terms of knowledge transfer and capture.[27]

Future of Technology-Based Learning

Chapter 4, "Technology-Based Learning (Trend 1)," described the first trend, technology-based learning, and its impact on the three different components of the learning process (individual, instruction design, and organization). The chapter also examined mobile learning. This is a huge field with serious implications on how organizations design learning activities and how individuals learn. However, there are several predictions that can be made or that have already manifested:

- **Popularity of mobile learning:** Mobile learning has the potential to become the "standard and normal" method of content delivery. It will be interesting to see the future of smaller mobile devices such as smartphones. However, as smartphones and tablets eventually merge to become smart tablets (this may be happening now), we may have a universal "learning tablet." Conversely, the security concerns associated with mobile devices will prevent the growth of mobile learning in certain industries. Mobile learning will support the idea of customization of learning, as discussed in Chapter 6, "Customized Learning and Learner Control (Trend 3)." That is, mobile learning will encourage individuals to customize learning environments to suit their needs.

- **Blended learning may be the answer:** Blended learning has the potential to become the preferred approach to designing electronic learning activities, but it is expensive.[28] In addition, blended learning environments can be used to suit the needs of learners and can provide them with considerable control over the learning process.

- **The return of traditional, face-to-face instructional environments:** It is possible that the traditional, face-to-face instructional environment will find a unique place in the learning space. We know it works—we have seen the results.

The traditional, face-to-face instructional environment will be referred to as a "premium learning product," offered only to a select few learners based on their needs and available resources. This premium learning product will be taught by the best instructors or trainers and will use learning technologies as complementary tools.

- **Quality of social learning:** The future of social learning will be fascinating. People will eventually realize that all interpersonal interactions, whether virtual or in person, are not the same, and there are only limited "quality" interactions that can occur in a day or at a given time. Individuals will select the type of interactions they would like to have with others. The quality of the interaction (not quantity) is likely to become extremely important.

- **Relevant learning content:** The learner of the future will have limited time to focus on learning. The quality of learning content becomes more important than the quantity of content. Learning content will have to be creative and include games and interactive features.[29]

Future of Informal Learning

Chapter 5, "Informal Learning (Trend 2)," discussed the second trend of informal learning. It described the different types of informal learning, introduced the idea of *informal learning strategy,* and described the characteristics of individuals most likely to participate in informal learning. Some of the futuristic trends include

- **Flexibility:** Informal learning has the potential to grow exponentially in the future as individuals have less time for formalized learning. Informal learning will become popular as jobs/work become more flexible, mobile, and collaborative.

- **Formalized to guide the learner:**[30] Organizations are more likely to provide some structure to informal learning by providing detailed guidelines to individuals on how to learn informally. The goal here will be to prevent individuals from wasting time and from acquiring unnecessary competencies. However, this has to be done with caution; too much structure may make informal learning into something that it is not supposed to be, as there's a fine line between informal and formal learning.

- **Learning outcomes:**[31] One of the challenges of informal learning is to evaluate the learning that takes place. Organizations are more likely to develop formal evaluation methods to determine the quantity and the quality of learning that occurs from informal learning activities.

Future of Customized Learning and Learner Control

Chapter 6 discussed the importance of customized learning and learner control. The chapter described customized learning, the various types of instructional designs, and different individual characteristics.

- **Fit between learner and instructional design:**[32] An important idea discussed in the chapter was the notion of the fit between instructional design and individual characteristics to maximize learning and behavioral changes. As mentioned in Chapter 6, given the high cost of developing employees (such as financial costs and emotional costs), it is important to identify individuals most likely to benefit from participating in learning activities. It is likely that organizations will include individual characteristics in any selection program for training and development. In addition, building on the idea of fit, customization of learning is likely to become a standard practice, especially for high-potential employees.

- **More learner control:**[33] The idea of providing the learner with more control over the learning process has been around for a while, but it is likely to become more prominent in the near future. This is analogous to smartphones or smart tablets. The user of the smartphone or a smart mobile device decides what applications to select or not select, and which to let go. In the smartphone world, this is considered a positive user experience. The same process can be applied to the training and development world. In the future, the learner will have a choice to select what to learn, where to learn, and when to learn. In other words, learners will have extreme control over their learning process. Nonetheless, it is important to keep in mind that the design process—that is, how instructional content is developed and organized—is most likely to remain under the control of professionals, such as instructional designers, instructors, and trainers.

Future of Continuous Learning

Chapter 7, "Continuous Learning (Trend 4)," examined the fourth trend of continuous learning. This chapter described continuous learning, explained reasons for continuous learning, and described strategies that organizations and individuals can use to continuously learn.

Some of the future trends include the following:

- **Need for continuous learning:**[34] Similar to other concepts discussed earlier, continuous learning is most likely to become a requirement for both organizations and individuals. For the individual, continuous learning will become a necessity as an important tool that an individual has to compete in the knowl-edge-intensive labor markets. This is especially true, keeping in mind that knowledge and information constantly keep on increasing and changing.

- **Strategic alliances:** To respond to the pressures of continuous learning, organizations are likely to seek the help of educational institutions and experts to develop curriculum that is consis-tent with the idea of continuous learning. For example, busi-ness schools and corporate learning functions can collaborate to develop learning initiatives.

- **Identifying continuous learners:**[35] There is likely to be an increase in the development of reliable and valid assessment techniques to identify continuous learners, especially identify-ing the characteristics, attitudes, and motivations of continuous learners.

Future of Learning and Development through Teamwork

Chapter 8, "Learning and Development through Teamwork (Trend 5)," discussed the fifth trend of development and learning that occurs through teamwork. This chapter described different types of teams and how teams work, the characteristics of successful teams and effective team members, and the importance of collaborative learning. There are two important themes:

- **Virtual teams:**[36] Team-based learning is most likely to revolve around virtual teams, especially virtual teams that are geograph-ically apart. Virtual teams will continue to increase in popularity in the near future.

- **Multicultural teams:**[37] Similar to virtual teams, multicultural teams are likely to continue to grow in the near future. Training programs like cross-cultural training and diversity training will become extremely useful to help individuals to successfully work in teams that include members from different cultures and ethnic backgrounds.

Future of Extreme Development

Chapter 9, "Extreme Development: Stretch Assignments and Learning Agility (Trend 6)," discussed the sixth trend of extreme development. The chapter described the concepts of development and extreme development. It then discussed the importance of stretch assignments and learning agility.

Some of the trends in the future might include:

- **Selection and customization:** Organizations are more inclined to focus on identifying the characteristics of individuals most likely to benefit from learning activities that use extreme development such as stretch assignments. In addition, customization of learning activities becomes relevant here. In other words, extreme development will probably be customized to suit individual needs and characteristics.

- **More inclusive:**[38] Traditionally, extreme development activities have been reserved for the most talented or high-potential employees. It is likely that in the future, organizations may take a more inclusive approach and offer extreme development to employees at different levels of the organization. This approach may become popular in industries with serious shortages of talent.

Future of the New Experts

Chapter 10, "The New Experts (Trend 7)," discussed the final trends—the new experts. This chapter described experts, explained how experts are developed, and described the role of reverse knowledge transfer with experts. There are three important themes here:

- **More experts:** The number of experts at all levels of the organization is more likely to increase in the future, as jobs become more specialized, mobile, and complex than in the past. It seems that to maintain job security, individuals will be required to specialize in areas of established expertise.

- **Ownership of expertise:** Individuals will have to proactively manage their expertise and think and behave like entrepreneurs. This will involve being passionate about their specialization and successfully marketing and selling their expertise. In addition, experts will have to constantly update and maintain their competencies and be on the lookout for the next big expertise in the relevant area.

- **Managing distractions and information overload:** With the advent of information technologies, it is possible experts are more prone to distractions and information overload. Thus, it is imperative that individuals who are on the path of developing expertise learn how to manage information overload and develop strong filters to distinguish between relevant and irrelevant knowledge.

Future of Investments in Workforce Learning and Development

Finally, Chapter 11, "Investment in Workforce Learning and Development," discussed investment in workforce development.

This chapter described the investment perspective, the importance of developing a corporate learning strategy, and the importance of having a dedicated talent management function. In addition, the chapter described the role of evaluation of investments in workforce development.

Future trends in this area include the following:

- **Learning is a significant part of talent management:** More and more organizations are realizing that to be successful, the learning function has to be strategic, which means it has to be tied to the organization's overall talent management strategy. It is likely that for organizations that are effective in attracting, retaining, and developing talent, the learning function is highly integrated with the talent management function in an organization. The chief learning officer (CLO) is an example of a position that exists in organizations that consider talent development as a strategic priority.

- **Impact on the bottom line:**[39] There is considerable focus on examining the impact of learning on the bottom line. Organizations will continue to use workforce analytics and advanced learning metrics to make learning extremely transparent and measure learning in real time. Over time, this approach is likely to make learning more efficient and learners more agile.

- **Learner segmentation:** Similar to the notion of workforce differentiation,[40] organizations are likely to categorize learners into different groups based on potential, learning needs, talent, and available resources. More and more organizations will try to offer the right learning, to the right learner, at the right time.

Conclusion

It is clear that the seven trends discussed in this book are changing workplace training and development in significant ways. These changes will continue to evolve in the near future and stimulate growth in the field of learning and development. The knowledge economy is not going away. Technology-based learning is here to stay. Jobs are changing constantly. Turnover is now rapid and becoming a new reality. Talent shortages are becoming more apparent in almost every industry. Put all of this together and we have a recipe for rapid and constant change.

Happy Learning!

A

Case-Study Examples

This appendix lists selected examples of case studies discussed in the chapters.

Globalization Technology and Global Leadership Development in Nissan Motor Company

Related to Chapters 1, 4, and 9

Source/Adapted from: Lang, Annamarie. (2013). Accelerate the Leadership Engine. Chief Learning Officer, April, 42–47.

Nissan is a global company that employs more than 150,000 people and has markets in more than 160 countries. With this geographically diverse spread of employees and customers, there was a need for Nissan to develop its high-potential leaders so that they could help the company grow in markets worldwide. Although these high potentials were working on different continents and had different levels of language proficiencies and skills, Nissan management sought to introduce a curriculum that would foster similar leadership skills based on the core values of the business. Nissan ultimately teamed up with the management consulting company, Development Dimensions International (DDI), to build a standardized set of leadership vocabulary that could be used throughout Nissan operations. The program also featured courses that honed in on building relationships, giving feedback, and encouraging interaction with fellow high potentials; due to the challenges of distance, these courses were not conducted in-person but were implemented virtually. Learners, therefore, could connect through the Web and access training courses, learning labs, and personalized feedback as well as interact with others across the globe through role-plays and team exercises. After Nissan's first group of high potentials finished the program in 2010, management found that there was an improvement in desired behavior changes and participants learned more about the roles that other members played in their respective countries.

Coaching and Knowledge Transfer

Related to Chapters 3, 7, and 9

Source/Adapted from: Lawson, John. (2012). The Leader as a Coach. Chief Learning Officer, June, 72–76.

For industrial supply distributor W. W. Grainger, Inc., coaching is a pivotal part of the learning process. At Grainger's "Leader as Coach" leadership program, high-performing managers participate in a 10-day curriculum that helps align them to the goals of the company and helps to boost performance through interactions with senior executives. In the planning stages of this program, interviews were conducted with senior leaders to grasp a better understanding of what the desired outcomes of the program should be. The executives continued to play a major role throughout the course of the program. Senior leaders created a video in which they shared their best coaching strategies and conversations; this video is then shown to trainees early in the "Leader as Coach" process. Upon completion of the program, these experienced executives then give recognition and credit to those managers who demonstrate the desired behaviors and successes—it is a system of support. This program, therefore, allows senior employees to impart their coaching skills to the participating managers to cultivate a greater community of leaders and coaches. Ultimately, the development team found that the program has a substantial impact on the participants and helps to improve their communication and coaching skills.

Developing Experts at FM Global

Related to Chapters 6 and 10

Source/Adapted from: Freedman, Karen. (2013). Experiencing Risk, Hands-On. Chief Learning Officer, March, 42–48.

FM Global, a commercial property insurer that concentrates on engineering principles, has a commitment to developing its engineers to ensure they can protect insured properties all over the world. The SimZone was created at FM Global to serve as an experiential classroom that simulates real-life situations, such as fire, electrical risks, and equipment hazards. By generating thousands of property risk simulations, the SimZone provides a hands-on training experience to participating engineers so that they can better solve property issues out in the field. To supplement this kind of simulated learning, FM Global development leaders have also made available training materials in the form of webinars, videos, and podcasts as well as a traditional classroom curriculum. With the introduction of the SimZone, engineers at FM Global have gained a greater knowledge of the different types of risk scenarios and are equipped to react effectively when crisis strikes. This has not only provided these engineers to be better prepared at work, but it has also encouraged the development of their expertise.

Endnotes

Chapter 1

1. Miller, L. (2012). 2012: ASTD State of the Industry Report: Organizations Continue to Invest in Workplace Learning. *T + D*, 66(11), 42–48.

2. The Very BEST Learning Organizations of 2013. (cover story). (2013). [Article]. *T+D*, 67(10), 34-82; Training Top 125. (2012). *Training*, 49(1), 66–107.

3. This categorization can be viewed as a way of organizing learning activities; however, it is possible that an activity can be used for both training and developmental purposes.

4. Briscoe, D. R., Schuler, R. S., & Tarique, I. (2012). *International Human Resource Management: Policies and Practices for Multinational Enterprises* (4th ed.). New York, NY: Routledge.

5. U.S. Department of Commerce, Bureau of Economic Analysis (2011 data). For more information, see http://www.bea.gov/newsreleases/international/mnc/2013/mnc2011.htm.

6. U.S. Department of Commerce, United States Census Bureau (2010–11 Data). For more information, see http://www.census.gov/foreign-trade/Press-Release/edb/2011/.

7. Foreign-Born Workers: Labor Force Characteristics (2012). Bureau of Labor Statistics, U.S. Department of Labor.

8. Camille, Ryan. (2013). *Language Use in the United States: 2011. American Community Survey Reports*. U.S. Department of Commerce, Economics and Statistics Administration, United States Census Bureau.

9. Harrison, J. K. (1994). Developing Successful Expatriate Managers: A Framework for t. *HR. Human Resource Planning, 17*(3), 17.

10. Ibid.

11. Hofstede, G. (2001). *Culture's Consequences International Differences in Work-Related Values*. California, USA: SAGE Publications, Inc.

12. United Nations Population Division, World Urbanization Prospects: The 2011 Revision (New York: UN, 2012).

13. Talent Shortage 2011 Survey Results, ManpowerGroup.

14. Talent Shortage 2012 Survey Results, ManpowerGroup.

15. Talent Shortage 2013 Survey Results, ManpowerGroup.

16. Based on Can Four Generations Focus in One Place? Demographics, Technology, and New Office Models Are Changing. (July 2013) The Conference Board KnowlEdge Series; Leading a Multigenerational Workforce. (2007) AARP; How to Effectively Manage a Multigenerational Workforce in the Federal Government. Four Generations Working Toward a Common Goal (2012), Deloitte; Leading a Multigenerational Workforce (2007), AARP; The Multigenerational Workforce: Opportunity for Competitive Success. (2009), Published by Society for Human Resource Management.

17. Toossi, Mitra. (2012). Labor Force Projections to 2020: A More Slowly Growing Workforce. Monthly Labor Review, Bureau of Labor Statistics.

18. Loretto, W., & White, P. (2006). Employers' Attitudes, Practices and Policies Towards Older Workers. *Human Resource Management Journal, 16*(3), 313–330. doi: 10.1111/j.1748-8583.2006.00013.x.

19. Calo, T. J. E. I.-C. P. (2008). Talent Management in the Era of the Aging Workforce: The Critical Role of Knowledge Transfer. *Public Personnel Management, 37*(4), 403–416.

20. Ibid.

21. Bureau of Labor Statistics, "The Employment Situation–Oct 2013."

22. Burns, Crosby, Barton, Kimberly, & Kerby, Sophia. (2012). The State of Diversity in Today's Workforce. As Our Nation Becomes More Diverse So Too Does Our Workforce, Center for American Progress; Bureau of Labor Statistics, "The Employment Situation–Oct 2013."

23. Ibid.

24. Bureau of Labor Statistics, "The Employment Situation–Oct 2013."

25. Ibid.

26. Tarique, I., & Schuler, R. S. (2010). Global Talent Management: Literature Review, Integrative Framework, and Suggestions for Further Research. [Article]. *Journal of World Business, 45*(2), 122–133. doi: 10.1016/j.jwb.2009.09.019.

27. Becker, B. E., Huselid, M. A., & Beatty, R. W. (2009). *The Differentiated Workforce: Transforming Talent into Strategic Impact*. Boston, Mass.: Harvard Business Press.

28. Lepak, D. P., & Snell, S. A. (2002). Examining the Human Resource Architecture: The Relationships Among Human Capital, Employment, and Human Resource Configurations. *Journal of Management, 28*(4), 517–543.

29. See Integrating Learning and Work Towards Maturity Benchmarking Practice 2012-13 Report – Executive Summary by Towards Maturity (www.towardsmaturity.com).

30. Mundey, Matt. (2010). Improving Competence and Compliance Through Self-Service and E-Learning Development. *Strategic HR REVIEW, 9*: 23–28.

Chapter 2

1. Based on the work of Gagne, R., & Medsker, K. (1996). *The Conditions of Learning*. Fort Worth, TX: Harcourt-Brace.

2. http://teachinglearningresources.pbworks.com/w/page/19919565/Learning%20Theories.

3. Ertmer, P. A., & Newby, T. J. (2013). Behaviorism, Cognitivism, Constructivism: Comparing Critical Features from an Instructional Design Perspective. [Article]. *Performance Improvement Quarterly, 26*(2), 43–71. doi: 10.1002/piq.21143.

4. This perspective is influenced by Jean Piaget, Lev Vygotsky, and Robert Gagne, among others.

5. Bower, G. H., & Hilgard, E. R. (1981). *Theories of Learning* (5th ed.). Englewood Cliffs, NJ: Prentice Hall.

6. Learning Theories, edited by Gayla Keesee. http://teachinglearningresources.pbworks.com/w/page/19919565/Learning%20Theories.

7. *How Do People Learn?* London, Chartered Institute of Personnel and Development, 2002.

8. Learning Theories, edited by Gayla Keesee. http://teachinglearningresources.pbworks.com/w/page/19919565/Learning%20Theories.

9. This perspective is heavily influenced by the work of B. F. Skinner, Ivan Pavlov, John Watson, and Edward Thorndike, among others.

10. *How Do People Learn?* London, Chartered Institute of Personnel and Development, 2002.

11. Ibid.

12. Ibid.

13. Ibid.

14. Bandura, A. (1977). *Social Learning Theory*. Englewood Cliffs, NJ: Prentice Hall.

15. Bandura, A. (1977a). *Social Learning Theory.* Englewood Cliffs, NJ: Prentice Hall; Black, S., & Mendenhall, M. (1990). Cross-Cultural Training Effectiveness: A Review and Theoretical Framework. *Academy of Management Review, 15,* 113–136.

16. Blanchard, N., Thacker. J., & Blanchard, N. (2003). *Effective Training: Systems, Strategies and Practices* (2nd ed.). NJ: Prentice Hall.

17. *Social Learning Theory.* Englewood Cliffs, NJ: Prentice Hall; Black, J. S., & Mendenhall, M. (1990). Cross-Cultural Training Effectiveness: A Review and A Theor. Academy of Management. *The Academy of Management Review, 15*(1), 113–113; Noe, R. A. (2008). *Employee Training and Development* (4th ed.). New York, NY: McGraw-Hill/Irwin.

18. Ibid.

19. Black, S., & Mendenhall, M. (1990). Cross-Cultural Training Effectiveness: A Review and Theoretical Framework. *Academy of Management Review, 15,* 113–136.

20. Bandura, A. (1997). *Self-Efficacy: The Exercise of Control.* New York: W. H. Freeman and Company; Bandura, A. (1977). Self-Efficacy: Toward a Unifying Theory of Behavior Change. *Psychological Review, 84,* 191–215.

21. This perspective is influenced by John Dewey, Jean Piaget, and Lev Vygotsky, among others.

22. Prince, M., & Felder, Richard. (2006). Inductive Teaching and Learning Methods: Definition, Comparisons, and Research Bases. *Journal of Engr. Education, 95* (2), 123–138.

23. How do people learn and The Change Agenda. The Chartered Institute of Personnel and Development, 2002: www.cipd.co.uk.

24. Altman, Brian. (2009). Determining US Workers' Training: History and Constructivist Paradigm. *Journal of European Industrial Training, 33,* 480–491.

25. Knowles, M. S., Holton, E. F., & Swanson, R. A. (2011). *The Adult Learner: The Definitive Classic in Adult Education and Human Resource Development* (7th ed.). Amsterdam; Boston: Elsevier.

26. Ibid.

27. How do people learn and The Change Agenda. The Chartered Institute of Personnel and Development, 2002: www.cipd.co.uk.

28. The idea of high-performance learning systems is based on the notion of high-performance work systems. See Huselid, M. A. (1995). The Impact of Human Resource Management Practices on Turnover, Productivity, and Corporate Financial Performance. *Academy of Management Journal, 38*, 635–673; 1. Boxall, P. (2012). High-Performance Work Systems: What, Why, How and for Whom? *Asia Pacific Journal of Human Resources, 50*, 169.

29. Tarique, I., & Schuler, R. S. (2010). Global Talent Management: Literature Review, Integrative Framework, and Suggestions for Further Research. [Article]. *Journal of World Business, 45*(2), 122-133. doi: 10.1016/j.jwb.2009.09.019.

30. Noe, R. A. (1986). Trainees' Attributes and Attitudes: Neglected Influences on Training Effectiveness. *Academy of Management. The Academy of Management Review, 11*(4), 736.

31. Beier, Margaret, & Kanfer, Ruth. (2010). Motivation in Training and Development: Phase Perspective. In Steve Kozlowski & Eduardo Salas (Eds). *Learning, Training, Development in Organizations*, New York: Taylor & Francis Group.

32. See Colquitt, J. A., LePine, J. A., & Noe, R. A. (2000). Toward an Integrative Theory of Training Motivation: A Meta-Analytic Path Analysis of 20 Years of Research. *Journal of Applied Psychology, 85*(5), 678-707.

33. Buss A. (1989). Personality as Traits. *American Psychologist, 44*, 1378–1388.

34. Costa, P., & McCrae, R. (1992). Normal Personality Assessment in Clinical Practice: The NEO Personality Inventory. *Psychological Assessment, 4,* 5–13.

35. Tarique, I. (2005). International executive development: The influence of international developmental activities, personality, and early international experience on success in global work activities. (Order No. 3160328, Rutgers The State University of New Jersey - New Brunswick). ProQuest Dissertations and Theses.

36. Gully, S. M., & Chen, G. (2010). Individual Differences, Attribute-Treatment Interactions, and Training Outcomes. In S. W. J. Kozlowski & E. Salas (Eds.), Learning, Training, and Development in Organizations (pp. 3-64). SIOP Organizational Frontiers Series. San Francisco, CA: Jossey-Bass.

37. Noe, R. A. (2008). *Employee Training and Development* (4th ed.). New York, NY: McGraw-Hill/Irwin.

38. Gully, S. M., & Chen, G. (2010). Individual Differences, Attribute-Treatment Interactions, and Training Outcomes. In S. W. J. Kozlowski & E. Salas (Eds.), Learning, Training, and Development in Organizations (pp. 3-64). SIOP Organizational Frontiers Series. San Francisco, CA: Jossey-Bass.

39. Rotter, J. B. (1990). Internal Versus External Control of Reinforcement: A Case History of a Variable. *American Psychologist, 45*(4), 489-493. doi: 10.1037/0003-066x.45.4.489.

40. Examples of learning styles include Myers–Briggs, Honey and Mumford's Typology, and Kolb's Learning-Style Inventory.

41. Osland, J., Kolb, D. A., & Rubin, I. M. (2001). *Organizational Behavior: An Experiential Approach* (7th ed.). Upper Saddle River, NJ: Prentice Hall; Kolb, D. A. (1984). *Experiential Learning: Experience as the Source of Learning and Development*. Englewood Cliffs, NJ: Prentice Hall.

42. Fragmented learning has been discussed in a variety of contexts; see Dennis, E. E., Meyer, P., & Sundar, S. (2003). Learning Reconsidered: Education in the Digital Age:

Communications, Convergence and the Curriculum. *Journalism & Mass Communication Educator*, 57(4), 292-317.; Drucker, P. F., Dyson, E., Handy, C., Saffo, P., & Senge, P. M. (1997). Looking Ahead: Implications of the Present. (cover story). *Harvard Business Review*, 75(5), 18–32.; Humphrey, D. (2005). Why Integrative Learning? Why Now? *Peer Review*, 7(4), 30-31. Fletcher, G. H., & Wooddell, G. D. (1976). *The Future, as Process.*; Kim, D. H. (1994). Do organizations learn? Chemtech, 24(9), 14; Simonin, B. L. (1997). The Importance of Collaborative Know-How: An Empirical Test of the Learning Organization. *Academy Of Management Journal*, 40(5), 1150-1174; Crossan, M. M., Maurer, C. C., & White,
R. E. (2011). Reflections on the 2009 AMR Decade Award: Do We have a Theory of Organizational Learning? Academy Of Management Review, 36(3), 446–460. In this section I discuss this concept at the individual level.

43. Weisser, L. (2012). Facing the Future: What Skills Will Your Employees Need? [Article]. *Canadian Learning Journal*, 16(1), 23-25; Neubert, G. A., & Binko, J. B. (1991). Using the Inductive Approach to Construct Content Knowledge. *Teacher Educator*, 27(1), 31–37.

44. Bower, G. H., & Hilgard, E. R. (1981). *Theories of Learning* (5th ed.). Englewood Cliffs, NJ: Prentice Hall.

Chapter 3

1. DeNisi, A. S., Hitt, M. A., & Jackson, S. E. (2003). "The Knowledge-Based Approach to Sustainable Competitive Advantage." In Jackson, S. E., Hitt, M. A., & DeNisi A. S. (Eds.), *Managing Knowledge for Sustained Competitive Advantage: Designing Strategies for Effective Human Resource Management*. SIOP Frontiers Series. San Francisco: Jossey Bass (pp. 3–36).

2. Argote, L., & Ingram, P. (2000). "Knowledge Transfer: A Basis for Competitive Advantage in Firms." *Organizational Behavior and Human Decision Processes, 82*(1): 150–169; Jackson, S. E., Hitt, M. A., and DeNisi, A. S. (eds.) (2003). *Managing Knowledge for Sustained Competitive Advantage: Designing Strategies for Effective Human Resource Management*. San Francisco: Jossey-Bass.

3. Origins of a knowledge economy can be traced back to Drucker, Peter. (1969). *The Age of Discontinuity: Guidelines to Our Changing Society*. New York: Harper and Row.

4. I build on the work of Harrison, Rosemary, & Kessels, Joseph. (2003). *Human Resource Development in a Knowledge Economy*. Hampshire: Palgrave Macmillan, UK.

5. See Brinkley, Ian. (2006). Defining the Knowledge Economy. Knowledge Economy Program Report. Published by the Work Foundation, London, UK; Harrison, Rosemary, & Kessels, Joseph. (2003). *Human Resource Development in a Knowledge Economy*. Location: Palgrave Macmillan, UK.

6. Harrison, Rosemary, & Kessels, Joseph. (2003). *Human Resource Development in a Knowledge Economy*. Hampshire: Palgrave Macmillan, UK.

7. Ibid.

8. Briscoe, D. R., Schuler, R. S., & Tarique, I. (2012). *International Human Resource Management: Policies and Practices for Multinational Enterprises* (4th ed.). New York, NY: Routledge.

9. Ibid.

10. Drucker, P. F. (1996). *Landmarks of Tomorrow: A Report on the New "Post-Modern" World*. New Brunswick, NJ: Transaction Publishers; Drucker, P. F. (1959). *Landmarks of Tomorrow* (1st ed.). New York: Harper.

11. Redpath, L., Hurst, D., & Devine, K. (2007). Contingent Knowledge Worker Challenges. [Article]. *Human Resource Planning, 30*(3), 33–38.

12. Szulanski, G. (1996). Exploring Internal Stickiness: Impediments to the Transfer of Best Practice Within the Firm. *Strategic Management Journal, 17*(Winter Special Issue): 27–43.

13. Bohn, Rogers, & Short, James. (2012). Measuring Consumer Information. *International Journal of Communication 6,* 980–1000.

14. Natchez, Meryl. (2009). Information Overload. *T+D, 63,* 4.

15. Brennan, L. L. (2011). The Scientific Management of Information Overload. [Article]. *Journal of Business & Management, 17*(1), 121–134.

16. de Bakker, S. (2007 2007 Annual Meeting). *Information Overload Within Organizational Settings: Exploring the Causes of Overload.*

17. Berthoin Antal, A., Stroo, I., & Willems, M. (n.d.) Drawing on the Knowledge of Returned Expatriates for Organizational Learning. Case Studies in German Multinational Companies. FS II 00-104. Available online at www.wz-berlin.de/~abantal; Lazarova, M., & Tarique, I. (2005). Knowledge Transfer upon Repatriation. *Journal of World Business, 40*(4), 361–373.

18. Lazarova, M., & Tarique, I. (2005). Knowledge Transfer upon Repatriation. *Journal of World Business, 40*(4), 361–373.

19. Blanchard, N., & Thacker, J. W. (1999). *Effective Training Systems, Strategies, and Practices.* Upper Saddle River, NJ: Prentice Hall.

20. Lazarova, M., & Tarique, I. (2005). Knowledge Transfer upon Repatriation. *Journal of World Business, 40*(4), 361–373.

Chapter 4

1. Sloman, M. (2009). Learning and Technology—What Have We Learnt? *Impact: Journal of Applied Research in Workplace E-Learning, 1*(1), 12-26.

2. Reiser, R. (2001). A History of Instructional Design and Technology: Part 1: A History of Instructional Media. *Educational Technology Research and Development, 49*(1): 1042–1629.

3. Sloman, M. (2009). Learning and Technology—What Have We Learnt? *Impact: Journal of Applied Research in Workplace E-Learning, 1*(1), 12–26.

4. Wilson, Charles, Orellana, Marvin, & Meek, Miki. (2010). The Learning Machines, New York Times, http://www.nytimes.com/interactive/2010/09/19/magazine/classroom-technology.html?hp&_r=0.

5. Based on 2013 State of the Industry by The American Society for Training & Development (ASTD) and the 2013 Training Industry Report, Training. www.trainingmag.com.

6. 2013 Training Industry Report, Training. www.trainingmag.com.

7. 2013 State of the Industry by The American Society for Training & Development (ASTD).

8. Ibid.

9. Cabage, N., & Zhang, S. (2013). Web 3.0 Has Begun. *Interactions, 20*(5), 26; and Leibtag, A. (2012). Three Reasons the Web Is Morphing into Web 3.0. *EContent, 35*(10), 11.

10. Brack, Jessica. (2010). Unlocking the Potential of On-Demand Learning in the Workplace. UNC Executive Development.

11. Cannon-Bowers, J. A., & Bowers, C. (2010). Synthetic Learning Environments: On Developing a Science of Simulation, Games, and Virtual Worlds for Training. In Learning, Training, and Development in Organizations, edited by S. Koslowski and E. Salas. Mahwah, NJ: Lawrence Erlbaum Associates.

12. Ibid.

13. Paharia, Rajat. (2012). "Enterprise Gamification: The Gen Y Factor" white paper. Bunchball – Gamification Blog.

14. See Ryan, Marco, Sleigh, Andy, Soh, Kai Wee, & Li, Zed. (2013). Why Gamification Is a Serious Business. Outlook by Accenture: http://www.accenture.com/SiteCollectionDocuments/PDF/Accenture-Outlook-Why-gamification-is-serious-business.pdf.

15. Cannon-Bowers, J. A., & Bowers, C. (2010). Synthetic Learning Environments: On Developing a Science of Simulation, Games, and Virtual Worlds for Training. In Learning, Training, and Development in Organizations, edited by S. Koslowski and E. Salas. Mahwah, NJ: Lawrence Erlbaum Associates.

16. Fleck, J. (2012). Blended learning and learning communities: opportunities and challenges. *The Journal of Management Development, 31*(4), 398–411. doi: http://dx.doi.org/10.1108/02621711211219059.

17. Hovis, S. (2012). Developing Capable Leaders Through Blended Learning. *T + D, 66*(5), 76–77.

18. Measuring the Information Society. (2013). International Telecommunication Union.

19. 2013 Learning & Development Technology Report. Impact Instruction Group. http://www.impactinstruction.com/.

20. See Kukulska-Hulme, A., & Traxler, J. (2005). Mobile Learning: A Handbook for Educators and Trainers. New York: Routledge Falmer.

21. Implementing Mobile Learning. 5 Key Steps to Make the Right Strategic Decisions. Kineo. http://www.kineo.com/m/0/learning-insights-2013.pdf.

22. Brink, Julie. (2011). M-Learning: The Future of Technology, *T+D, 65*: 27–29.

23. Implementing Mobile Learning. 5 Key Steps to Make the Right Strategic Decisions. Kineo. http://www.kineo.com/m/0/learning-insights-2013.pdf.

24. Lahiri, M., & Moseley, J. L. (2012). Is Mobile Learning the Future of 21st Century Education? Educational Considerations from Various Perspectives. *Educational Technology*, 52(4), 3–13; and Brink, Julie. (2011). M-Learning: The Future of Technology, *T+D*, 65: 27–29.

25. Safeguarding, Security and Privacy in Mobile Education. GSMA Connected Living Programme: mEducation, March 2012. http://www.gsma.com/.

26. See Going Mobile. Create Practices that Transform Learning. A white paper by ASTD Research. (2013). Volume 5, No 1.

27. Implementing Mobile Learning. 5 Key Steps to Make the Right Strategic Decisions. Kineo. http://www.kineo.com/m/0/learning-insights-2013.pdf.

Chapter 5

1. The 70:20:10 model was developed by Michael M. Lombardo and Robert W. Eichinger based on their research with the Center for Creative Leadership. See Lombardo, Michael M., & Eichinger, Robert W. (1996). *The Career Architect Development Planner* (1st ed.). Minneapolis: Lominger.

2. See Informal Learning. The Social Revolution. White paper, ASTD Research, Vol 4, No 3, 2013.

3. Ibid.

4. Knowles, M. (1950). *Informal Adult Education*. New York: Association Press, cited in Kim, S., & McLean, G. N. (2014). The Impact of National Culture on Informal Learning in the Workplace. [Article]. *Adult Education Quarterly*, 64(1), 39–59. doi: 10.1177/0741713613504125. Also see Knowles, M. S., Holton, E. F., & Swanson, R. A. (2011). *The Adult Learner* (7th ed.). Amsterdam; Boston: Elsevier.

5. See Le Clus, M. (2011). Informal Learning in the Work-place: A Review of the Literature. *Australian Journal of Adult Learning, 51*(2), 355–373; Colley, Helen, Hodkinson, Phil, & Malcom, Janice. (2002). Non-Formal Learning: Mapping the Conceptual Terrain. A Consultation Report. Leeds: University of Leeds Lifelong Learning Institute. Also available in *the informal education archives*: http://www.infed.org/archives/e-texts/colley_informal_learning.htm.

6. Marsick, V. J., & Watkins, K. E. (1990). Informal and Incidental Learning in the Workplace. New York: Routledge; Marsick, Victoria J., & Watkins, Karen E. (2001). *Informal and Incidental Learning. In New Directions for Adult and Continuing Education.* San Francisco: Jossey-Bass, A Publishing Unit of John Wiley & Sons, Inc.; Whimbey, A. E., Mechanic, A., & Ryan, S. F. (1968). Individual Difference in Incidental Learning and Intentional Learning. *The Journal of Psychology, 70,* 77–80; Countee, S. F. (2006). Intentional Learning: A Foundation for Lifelong Learning and Continuing Competence. *OT Practice, 11*(13), 12–14.

7. Weinstein, Margery. (2013). Regulating Informal Learning, trainingmag.com. http://www.trainingmag.com/content/regulating-informal-learning.

8. Based on Weinstein, M. (2013). Regulating Informal Learning. *Training.* Retrieved from http://www.trainingmag.com/content/regulating-informal-learning; Informal Learning: The Social Evolution, Whitepaper, Vol 4, No 3 by ASTD Research (2013);Leslie, B. (1997). Informal Learning: The New Frontier of Employee & Organizational Development. [Article]. *Economic Development Review, 15*(4), 12; Eraut, M. (2004). Informal Learning in the Workplace. *Studies in Continuing Education, 26*(2), 247–273; Paradise, A. (2008). Informal Learning: Overlooked or Overhyped? *T + D, 62*(7), 52–53, 56.

9. Weinstein, M. (2013). Regulating Informal Learning. *Training*. Retrieved from http://www.trainingmag.com/content/regulating-informal-learning; Tannenbaum, S. I., Beard, R. L., McNall, L. A., & Salas, E. (2010). Informal Learning and Development in Organizations. In Kozlowski, S. W. J., & Salas, E. (Eds.), *Learning, Training, and Development in Organizations*. (pp. 303-331). New York: Routledge/Taylor & Francis Group.

10. Ibid.

11. Ibid.

12. Eraut, M. (2004). Informal Learning in the Workplace. *Studies in Continuing Education, 26*(2), 247–273.

13. Tannenbaum, S. I., Beard, R. L., McNall, L. A., & Salas, E. (2010). Informal Learning and Development in Organizations. In Kozlowski, S. W. J., & Salas, E. (Eds.), *Learning, Training, and Development in Organizations*. (pp. 303-331). New York: Routledge/Taylor & Francis Group.

14. Paradise, A. (2008b). Informal Learning: Overlooked or Overhyped? [Article]. *T+D, 62*(7), 52–53.

Chapter 6

1. Miller, L. (2012). 2012: ASTD State of the Industry Report: Organizations Continue to Invest in Workplace Learning. *T + D, 66*(11), 42–48,46.

2. Caligiuri, P., & Tarique, I. (2009). Predicting Effectiveness in Global Leadership Activities. *Journal of World Business, 44*(3), 336; Gully, S. M., & Chen, G. (2010). Individual Differences, Attribute-Treatment Interactions, and Training Outcomes. In Kozlowski, S. W. J., & Salas, E. (Eds.). *Learning, Training, and Development in Organizations* (pp. 3–64). New York: Routledge/Taylor & Francis Group.

3. Snow, R. E. (1991). Aptitude-Treatment Interaction as a Framework for Research on Individual Differences in Psychotherapy. *Journal of Consulting and Clinical Psychology, 59*: 205–216.

4. Caligiuri, P., & Tarique, I. (2009). Predicting Effectiveness in Global Leadership Activities. *Journal of World Business, 44*(3), 336; Snow, R. E. (1991). Aptitude-Treatment Interaction as a Framework for Research on Individual Differences in Psychotherapy. *Journal of Consulting and Clinical Psychology, 59*: 205–216.

5. Gully, S. M., & Chen, G. (2010). Individual Differences, Attribute-Treatment Interactions, and Training Outcomes. In Kozlowski, S. W. J., & Salas, E. (Eds.). *Learning, Training, and Development in Organizations* (pp. 3–64). New York: Routledge/Taylor & Francis Group.

6. Kolb, D. A. (1984). *Experiential Learning: Experience as the Source of Learning and Development*. Englewood Cliffs, NJ: Prentice-Hall.

7. Caligiuri, P., & Tarique, I. (2009). Predicting Effectiveness in Global Leadership Activities. *Journal of World Business, 44*(3), 336.

8. Noe, R. A. (2010). *Employee Training and Development* (5th ed.). New York: McGraw-Hill Irwin.

9. Digman, J. (1990). Personality Structure: Emergence of the Five-Factor Model. *Annual Review of Psychology, 41*, 417-440; Costa, P., & McCrae, R. (1992). Normal Personality Assessment in Clinical Practice: The NEO Personality Inventory. *Psychological Assessment, 4*, 5–13.

10. Traditionalists, Baby Boomers, Generation X, Generation Y (and Generation Z) Working Together. What Matters and How They Learn? How Different Are They? Fact and Fiction. United Nations Joint Staff Pension Fund, Talent Management Team, New York Secretariat Headquarters.

11. Ibid.

12. El-Shamy, Susan. (2004). *How to Design and Deliver Training for the New and Emerging Generations*. San Francisco, CA: John Wiley and Sons; Traditionalists, Baby Boomers, Generation X, Generation Y (and Generation Z) Working Together. What Matters and How They Learn? How Different Are They? Fact and Fiction. United Nations Joint Staff Pension Fund, Talent Management Team, New York Secretariat Headquarters.

13. El-Shamy, Susan. (2004). *How to Design and Deliver Training for the New and Emerging Generations*. San Francisco, CA: John Wiley and Sons.

14. Traditionalists, Baby Boomers, Generation X, Generation Y (and Generation Z) Working Together. What Matters and How They Learn? How Different Are They? Fact and Fiction. United Nations Joint Staff Pension Fund, Talent Management Team, New York Secretariat Headquarters.

15. Ibid.

16. Ibid.

17. Cox, Tara. (2010). The Generation-Based Approach to Training. www.scrap.org.

18. Ibid.

19. Buss A. (1989). Personality as Traits. *American Psychologist 44*, 1378–1388; Costa, P., & McCrae, R. (1992). Normal Personality Assessment in Clinical Practice: The NEO Personality Inventory. *Psychological Assessment, 4*, 5–13.

20. Salas, E., & Cannon-Bowers, J. (2001). The Science of Training: A Decade of Progress. *Annual Review of Psychology, 52*, 471–499; Barrick, R., & Mount, K. (1991). The Big Five Personality Dimensions and Job Performance: A Meta-Analysis. *Personnel Psychology, 44*, 1–26.

21. Digman, J. (1990). Personality Structure: Emergence of the Five-Factor Model. *Annual Review of Psychology, 41*, 417–440; Goldberg, L. (1990). An Alternative "Description of

Personality": The Big Five Structure. *Journal of Personality and Social Psychology, 59,* 1216-1219; McCrae, R., & Costa, P. (1996). Toward a New Generation of Personality Theories: Theoretical Contexts for the Five-Factor Model. In Wiggins, J. (Ed.). *The Five-Factor Model of Personality: Theoretical Perspectives* (pp. 51–87). New York: Guilford.

22. Colquitt, J., LePine, J., & Noe, R. (2000). Toward an Integrative Theory of Training Motivation: A Meta-Analytic Path Analysis of 20 Years of Research. *Journal of Applied Psychology, 85:* 678–707; Caligiuri, P., & Tarique, I. (2009). Predicting Effectiveness in Global Leadership Activities. *Journal of World Business, 44*(3), 336.

23. Barrick, R., & Mount, K. (1991). The Big Five Personality Dimensions and Job Performance: A Meta-Analysis. *Personnel Psychology, 44,* 1–26; Costa, P., & McCrae, R. (1992). Normal Personality Assessment in Clinical Practice: The NEO Personality Inventory. *Psychological Assessment, 4,* 5–13; Caligiuri, P., & Tarique, I. (2006). International Assignee Selection and Cross-Cultural Training and Development. In Stahl, G. K., & Björkman, I. (Eds.). *Handbook of Research in International Human Resource Management* (pp. 302–322). Northampton, Mass.: Edward Elgar Publishing.

24. Herold, D., Davis, W., Fedor, D., & Parsons, C. (2002). Dispositional Influences on Transfer of Learning in Multistate Training Programs. *Personnel Psychology, 55,* 851–870; Caligiuri, P. (2000b). The Big Five Personality Characteristics as Predictors of Expatriate's Desire to Terminate the Assignment and Supervisor-Rated Performance. *Personnel Psychology, 53,* 67–88.

25. Caligiuri, P. (2000b). The Big Five Personality Characteristics as Predictors of Expatriate's Desire to Terminate the Assignment and Supervisor-Rated Performance. *Personnel Psychology, 53,* 67–88; Caligiuri, P., & Tarique, I. (2009). Predicting Effectiveness in Global Leadership Activities. *Journal of World Business, 44*(3), 336.

26. Orvis, K. A., Brusso, R. C., Wasserman, M. E., & Fisher, S. L. (2011). E-nabled for E-Learning? The Moderating Role of Personality in Determining the Optimal Degree of Learner Control in an E-Learning Environment. *Human Performance, 24*(1), 60–78. doi: 10.1080/08959285.2010.530633.

27. Barrick, R., & Mount, K. (1991). The Big Five Personality Dimensions and Job Performance: A Meta-Analysis. *Personnel Psychology, 44*, 1–26; Costa, P., & McCrae, R. (1992). Normal Personality Assessment in Clinical Practice: The NEO Personality Inventory. *Psychological Assessment, 4*, 5–13; De Raad, B., & Schouwenburg, H. (1996). Personality in Learning and Education: A Review. *European Journal of Personality, 10*, 303–336.

28. Graziano, W., Jensen-Campbell, L., & Hair, E. (1996). Perceiving Interpersonal Conflict and Reacting To It: The Case for Agreeableness. *Journal of Personality and Social Psychology, 70*, 820–835; Caligiuri, P. (2000a). Selecting Expatriates for Personality Characteristics: A Moderating Effect of Personality on the Relationship between Host National Contact and Cross-Cultural Adjustment. *Management International Review, 40*, 61-81.

29. Barrick, R., & Mount, K. (1991). The Big Five Personality Dimensions and Job Performance: A Meta-Analysis. *Personnel Psychology, 44*, 1–26; Costa, P., & McCrae, R. (1992). Normal Personality Assessment in Clinical Practice: The NEO Personality Inventory. *Psychological Assessment, 4*, 5–13; De Raad, B., & Schouwenburg, H. (1996). Personality in Learning and Education: A Review. *European Journal of Personality, 10*, 303-336.

30. Barrick, R., Mount, K., & Judge, T. (2001). Personality and Performance at the Beginning of the New Millennium: What Do We Know and Where Do We Go Next? *International Journal of Selection and Assessment, 9*, 9–30; Barrick, R., & Mount, K. (1991). The Big Five Personality Dimensions and

Job Performance: A Meta-Analysis. *Personnel Psychology, 44,* 1–26.

31. Colquitt, J., & Simmering, M. (1998). Conscientiousness, Goal Orientation, and Motivation to Learn During the Learning Process: A Longitudinal Study. *Journal of Applied Psychology,* 85, 678–707; Martocchio, J., & Judge, T. (1997). Relationships between Conscientiousness and Learning in Employee Training: Mediating Influences of Self-Deception and Self-Efficacy. *Journal of Applied Psychology,* 82, 764–773; Naquin, S., & Holton, E. (2002). The Effects of Personality, Affectivity, and Work Commitment on Motivation to Improve Work through Learning. *Human Resource Development Quarterly, 13,* 357–377.

32. Colquitt, J., & Simmering, M. (1998). Conscientiousness, Goal Orientation, and Motivation to Learn During the Learning Process: A Longitudinal Study. *Journal of Applied Psychology,* 85, 678–707; Kanfer, R., & Ackerman, P. (1989). Motivation and Cognitive Abilities: An Integrative/Aptitude-Treatment Interaction Approach to Skill Acquisition. *Journal of Applied Psychology, 74,* 657–690.

33. Costa, P., & McCrae, R. (1992). Normal Personality Assessment in Clinical Practice: The NEO Personality Inventory. *Psychological Assessment, 4,* 5–13; Caligiuri, P. (2000b). The Big Five Personality Characteristics as Predictors of Expatriate's Desire to Terminate the Assignment and Supervisor-Rated Performance. *Personnel Psychology, 53,* 67–88.

34. Caligiuri, P., & Tarique, I. (2009). Predicting Effectiveness in Global Leadership Activities. *Journal of World Business, 44*(3), 336.

35. Ibid.

36. Orvis, K. A., Brusso, R. C., Wasserman, M. E., & Fisher, S. L. (2011). E-nabled for E-Learning? The Moderating Role of Personality in Determining the Optimal Degree of Learner

Control in an E-Learning Environment. *Human Performance, 24*(1), 60–78. doi: 10.1080/08959285.2010.530633.

37. Barrick, R., & Mount, K. (1991). The Big Five Personality Dimensions and Job Performance: A Meta-Analysis. *Personnel Psychology, 44*, 1–26; Costa, P., & McCrae, R. (1992). Normal Personality Assessment in Clinical Practice: The NEO Personality Inventory. *Psychological Assessment, 4*, 5–13.

38. Caligiuri, P., Tarique, I., & Jacobs, R. (2009). Selection for International Assignments. *Human Resource Management Review, 19*(3), 251.

39. Noe, R. A. (2010). *Employee Training and Development* (5th ed.). New York: McGraw-Hill Irwin.

40. Gully, S. M., & Phillips, J. M. (2005). A Multilevel Application of Learning and Performance Orientations to Individual, Group, and Organizational Outcomes. In Martocchio, J. (Ed.). *Research in Personnel and Human Resource Management* (Vol. 24, pp. 1–52). Greenwich, CT: JAI Press.

41. Milheim, W. D., & Martin, B. L. (1991). Theoretical Bases for the Use of Learner Control: Three Different Perspectives. *Journal of Computer Based Instruction, 18*, 99–105; Ford, J. K., & Kraiger, K. (1995). The Application of Cognitive Constructs to the Instructional Systems Model of Training: Implications for Needs Assessment, Design and Transfer. In Cooper, C. L., & Robertson, I. T. (Eds.). *International Review of Industrial and Organizational Psychology* (pp. 1-48). Chichester, England: Wiley; Kay, Judy. (2001). Learner Control. *User Modeling and User-Adapted Interaction 11*: 111–127.

42. Ford, J. K., & Kraiger, K. (1995). The Application of Cognitive Constructs to the Instructional Systems Model of Training: Implications for Needs Assessment, Design and Transfer. In Cooper, C. L., & Robertson, I. T. (Eds.). *International Review of Industrial and Organizational Psychology* (pp. 1–48).

Chichester, England: Wiley; Milheim, W. D., & Martin, B. L. (1991). Theoretical Bases for the Use of Learner Control: Three Different Perspectives. *Journal of Computer Based Instruction, 18*, 99–105.

43. Ford, J., Smith, E. M., Weissbein, D. A., Gully, S. M., & Salas, E. (1998). Relationships of Goal Orientation, Metacognitive Activity, and Practice Strategies with Learning Outcomes and Transfer. *Journal of Applied Psychology, 83*(2), 218–233.

44. Orvis, K. A., Brusso, R. C., Wasserman, M. E., & Fisher, S. L. (2011). E-nabled for E-Learning? The Moderating Role of Personality in Determining the Optimal Degree of Learner Control in an E-Learning Environment. *Human Performance, 24*(1), 60–78. doi: 10.1080/08959285.2010.530633.

45. Ibid.

46. Kraiger, K., & Jerden, E. (2007). A Meta-Analytic Investigation of Learner Control: Old Findings and New Directions. In Fiore, S. M., & Salas, E. (Eds.). *Toward a Science of Distributed Learning* (pp. 65–90). Washington, DC: American Psychological Association.

47. Orvis, K. A., Brusso, R. C., Wasserman, M. E., & Fisher, S. L. (2011). E-nabled for E-Learning? The Moderating Role of Personality in Determining the Optimal Degree of Learner Control in an E-Learning Environment. *Human Performance, 24*(1), 60-78. doi: 10.1080/08959285.2010.530633.

48. Bell, B., & Kozlowski, S. (2008). Active Learning: Effects of Core Training Design Elements on Self-Regulatory Processes, Learning, and Adaptability. *Journal of Applied Psychology, 93*, 296–316.

Chapter 7

1. Tannenbaum, S. I. (1997). Enhancing Continuous Learning: Diagnostic Findings from Multiple Companies. *Human Resource Management, 36*(4), 437–452.

2. London, M., & Sessa, V. I. (2006). Group Feedback for Continuous Learning. *Human Resource Development Review,* 5(3), 303-329; Sessa, V. I., & London, M. (2005). *Continuous Learning in Organizations: Individual, Group, and Organizational Perspectives.* Mahwah, NJ: Lawrence Erlbaum; Molloy, J. C., & Noe, R. A. (2010). "Learning" a Living: Continuous Learning for Survival in Today's Talent Market. In Kozlowski, S. W. J., & Salas, E. (Eds.). *Learning, Training, and Development in Organizations* (pp. 333–361). New York: Routledge/ Taylor & Francis Group.

3. Molloy, J. C., & Noe, R. A. (2010). "Learning" a Living: Continuous Learning for Survival in Today's Talent Market. In Kozlowski, S. W. J., & Salas, E. (Eds.) *Learning, Training, and Development in Organizations* (pp. 33–361). New York: Routledge/Taylor & Francis Group.

4. Gratton, L. (2010). The Future of Work. *Business Strategy Review,* 21(3), 16–23; Gratton, L. (2011). Workplace 2025— What Will It Look Like? *Organizational Dynamics,* 40(4), 246–254; Levit, A. (2009). The Future World of Work: A Gen Xer's Perspective. [Opinion]. *Futurist,* 43(5), 39–39.

5. See Sessa, V. I., & London, M. (2005). *Continuous Learning in Organizations: Individual, Group, and Organizational Perspectives.* Mahwah, NJ: Lawrence Erlbaum; London, M., & Sessa, V. I. (2006). Group Feedback for Continuous Learning. *Human Resource Development Review,* 5(3), 303–329.

6. Tarique, I., & Schuler, R. S. (2010). Global Talent Management: Literature Review, Integrative Framework, and Suggestions for Further Research. *Journal of World Business,* 45(2), 122–133. doi: 10.1016/j.jwb.2009.09.019.

7. Senge, P. (1990), The Fifth Discipline: The Art & Practice of the Learning Organization, Doubleday Currency, New York, NY; Senge, P. (1990). The leader's new work: building learning organizations, Sloan Management Review, Vol. 32 No. 1, pp. 7–23; Gronhaug, K., & Stone, R. (2012). The learning organization. Competitiveness Review, 22(3), 261–275;

Filstad, C., & Gottschalk, P. (2011). Becoming a learning organization. The Learning Organization, 18(6), 486–500; Eijkman, H. (2011). The learning organization as concept and journal in the neo-millennial era. The Learning Organization, 18(3), 164–174.

8. Tannenbaum, S. I. (1997). Enhancing Continuous Learning: Diagnostic Findings from Multiple Companies. *Human Resource Management, 36*(4), 437–452.

9. Ibid.

10. Ibid.

11. Senge, P. (1990). *The Fifth Discipline*. New York: Doubleday/Currency.

12. For detailed information on learning organizations, see Senge, P. (1990). *The Fifth Discipline*. New York: Doubleday/Currency; Marquardt, M. J. (2002). *Building the Learning Organization* (2nd ed.). Palo Alto, CA: Davies-Black; Garvin, D. A., Edmondson, A. C., & Gino, F. (2008, 03). Is Yours a Learning Organization? *Harvard Business Review, 86*, 109–116.

13. Based on Molloy, J. C., & Noe, R. A. (2010). "Learning" a Living: Continuous Learning for Survival in Today's Talent Market. In Kozlowski, S. W. J., & Salas, E. (Eds.). *Learning, Training, and Development in Organizations* (pp. 333–361). New York: Routledge/Taylor & Francis Group.

14. Noe, R. A., & Wilk, S. L. (1993). Investigation of the Factors That Influence Employees' Participation in Development Activities. *Journal of Applied Psychology, 78*(2), 291; Maurer, T. J., & Tarulli, B. A. (1994). Investigation of Perceived Environment, Perceived Outcome, and Person Variables in Relationship to Voluntary Development Activity by Employees. *Journal of Applied Psychology, 79*(1), 3–14.

15. For a thorough review of the various factors, see the following works:

Maurer, T. J., & Chapman, E. F. (2013). Ten Years of Career Success in Relation to Individual and Situational Variables from the Employee Development Literature. *Journal of Vocational Behavior, 83*(3), 450.

Birdi, K., Allan, C., & Warr, P. (1997). Correlates and Perceived Outcomes of Four Types of Employee Development Activity. *Journal of Applied Psychology, 82*(6), 845–857.

Hurtz, G. M., & Williams, K. J. (2009). Attitudinal and Motivational Antecedents of Participation in Voluntary Employee Development Activities. *Journal of Applied Psychology, 94*(3), 635.

Maurer, T. J., & Tarulli, B. A. (1994). Investigation of Perceived Environment, Perceived Outcome, and Person Variables in Relationship to Voluntary Development Activity by Employees. *Journal of Applied Psychology, 79*(1), 3.

Noe, R. A., & Wilk, S. L. (1993). Investigation of the Factors That Influence Employees' Participation in Development Activities. *Journal of Applied Psychology, 78*(2), 291.

Van Vianen, A. E. M., Dalhoeven, B. A. G. W., & De Pater, I. E. (2011). Aging and Training and Development Willingness: Employee and Supervisor Mindsets. *Journal of Organizational Behavior, 32*(2), 226.

Zoogah, D. B. (2010). Why Should I Be Left Behind? Employees' Perceived Relative Deprivation and Participation in Development Activities. *Journal of Applied Psychology, 95*(1), 159.

London, M., & Smither, J. W. (1999). Career-Related Continuous Learning: Defining the Construct and Mapping the Process. In Ferris, G. E. (Ed.). *Research in Personnel and Human Resources Management* (pp. 81–122). Oxford: Elsevier.

16. Wright, K. (2013). Be a Lifelong Learner. *Training*. Retrieved from http://www.trainingmag.com/content/be-lifelong-learner.

17. Tharenou, P. (2001). Going Up? Do Traits and Informal Social Processes Predict Advancing in Management? *Academy of Management Journal, 44*: 1005–1017.

18. Knese, W. F. (2013). A Commitment to Continuous Learning. [Article]. *Strategic Finance, 95*(12), 6–61.

19. Maurer, T. J., & Weiss, E. M. (2010). Continuous Learning Skill Demands: Associations with Managerial Job Content, Age, and Experience. *Journal of Business and Psychology, 25*(1), 1–13. doi:10.1007/s10869-009-9126-0.

20. Rowold, J., & Schilling, J. (2006). Career-Related Continuous Learning. *Career Development International, 11*(6), 489–503. doi: http://dx.doi.org/10.1108/13620430610692917.

21. Baruch, Yehuda. (2004). *Managing Career. Theory and Practice*. UK: Prentice Hall.

22. Hurtz, G. M., & Williams, K. J. (2009). Attitudinal and Motivational Antecedents of Participation in Voluntary Employee Development Activities. *Journal of Applied Psychology, 94*(3), 635–653. doi:10.1037/a0014580.

23. Tannenbaum, S. I. (1997). Enhancing Continuous Learning: Diagnostic Findings from Multiple Companies. *Human Resource Management, 36*(4), 437–452.

24. Molloy, J. C., & Noe, R. A. (2010). "Learning" a Living: Continuous Learning for Survival in Today's Talent Market. In Kozlowski, S. W. J., & Salas, E. (Eds.). *Learning, Training, and Development in Organizations* (pp. 333–361). New York: Routledge/Taylor & Francis Group.

25. Caligiuri, P., & Tarique, I. (2009). Predicting Effectiveness in Global Leadership Activities. *Journal of World Business, 44*(3), 336.

26. Birdi, K., Allan, C., & Warr, P. (1997). Correlates and Perceived Outcomes of Four Types of Employee Development Activity. *Journal of Applied Psychology, 82*(6), 845–857.

Chapter 8

1. For examples, see Caligiuri, P. (2010). *Get a Life, Not a Job: Do What You Love and Let Your Talents Work for You*. Upper Saddle River, NJ: FT Press; The Future of Work. Changing How the World Works. www.oDesk.com.

2. London, M. (2013). Generative Team Learning in Web 2.0 Environments. *The Journal of Management Development*, 32(1), 73–95.

3. Katzenbach, J. R., & Smith, D. K. (1993). *The Wisdom of Teams: Creating the High-Performance Organization*. Boston: Harvard Business School Press.

4. SAS(R) High-Performance Marketing Optimization Takes on Big Analytics. (2012). *Marketing Weekly News*, 209.

5. Salas, E., Cooke, N. J., & Rosen, M. (2008). On Teams, Teamwork, and Team Performance: Discoveries and Developments. *Human Factors, 50*(3), 540–554.

6. Konopaske, Robert, & Ivancevich, John. (2004). *Global Management and Organizational Behavior*. New York: McGraw-Hill/Irwin.

7. Ibid.

8. Gomez-Mejia, L. R., Balkin, D. B., & Cardy, R. L. (2010). *Managing Human Resources*. Upper Saddle River, NJ: Prentice Hall.

9. Ibid.

10. Briscoe, D. R., Schuler, R. S., & Tarique, I. (2012). *International Human Resource Management: Policies and Practices for Multinational Enterprises* (4th ed.). New York: Routledge.

11. Ibid.

12. Ibid.

13. Cannon-Bowers, J. A., Tannenbaum, S. I., Salas, E., & Volpe, C. E. (1995). Defining Competencies and Establishing Team Training Requirements. In Guzzo, R., & Salas, E. (Eds.).

Team Effectiveness and Decision Making in Organizations (pp. 333–380). San Francisco, CA: Jossey-Bass; Also see Driskell, J. E., Goodwin, G. F., Salas, E., & O'Shea, P. (2006). What Makes a Good Team Player? Personality and Team Effectiveness. *Group Dynamics: Theory, Research, and Practice, 10*(4), 249–271. doi:10.1037/1089–2699.10.4.249.

14. Driskell, J. E., Goodwin, G. F., Salas, E., & O'Shea, P. (2006). What Makes a Good Team Player? Personality and Team Effectiveness. *Group Dynamics: Theory, Research, and Practice, 10*(4), 249–271.

15. Ibid.

16. Are You a Team Player? The Characteristics of an Effective Team Player. (2011). *Health Care Registration: The Newsletter for Health Care Registration Professionals, 20*(10), 8–9.

17. Ibid.

18. Ibid.

19. Lencioni, P. (2002). *The Five Dysfunctions of a Team: A Leadership Fable*. San Francisco, CA: Jossey-Bass.

20. Managing Teams (Pocket Mentor). (2010). Boston: Harvard Business Review Press.

21. London, M. (2013). Generative Team Learning in Web 2.0 Environments. *The Journal of Management Development, 32*(1), 73–95; London, M., & Sessa, V. I. (2007). How Groups Learn, Continuously. *Human Resource Management Journal, 46*(4), 651–669.

22. Ibid.

23. Ibid.

24. London, M. (2013). Generative Team Learning in Web 2.0 Environments. *The Journal of Management Development, 32*(1), 73–95.

25. Casse, P., & Banahan, E. (2011). 21st Century Team Skills. *Training Journal*, 11–16.

26. Briscoe, D. R., Schuler, R. S., & Tarique, I. (2012). *International Human Resource Management: Policies and Practices for Multinational Enterprises* (4th ed.). New York: Routledge.

27. Ibid.

28. Tjosvold, D., Yu, Z.-y., & Hui, C. (2004). Team Learning from Mistakes: The Contribution of Cooperative Goals and Problem-Solving. *The Journal of Management Studies, 41*(7), 1223–1245.

29. London, M., & Sessa, V. I. (2007). How Groups Learn, Continuously. *Human Resource Management Journal, 46*(4), 651–669.

30. London, M. (2013). Generative Team Learning in Web 2.0 Environments. *The Journal of Management Development, 32*(1), 73–95.

31. Ibid.

32. Ibid.

33. Cooke, N. J., & Fiore, S. (2010). Cognitively-Based Principles for the Design and Delivery of Training. In Kozlowski, S. W. J., & Salas, E. (Eds.). *Learning, Training, and Development in Organizations* (pp. 169–202). New York: Routledge, Taylor & Francis Group.

34. Ibid.

35. Park, S., Cho, Y., Yoon, S. W., & Han, H. (2013). Comparing Team Learning Approaches through the Lens of Activity Theory. *European Journal of Training and Development, 37*(9), 788–810.

Chapter 9

1. Noe, R. A., & Wilk, S. L. (1993). Investigation of the Factors That Influence Employees' Participation in Development Activities. *Journal of Applied Psychology, 78*(2), 291.

2. Maurer, T. J., & Tarulli, B. A. (1994). Investigation of Perceived Environment, Perceived Outcome, and Person Variables in Relationship to Voluntary Development Activity by Employees. *Journal of Applied Psychology, 79*(1), 3–14.

3. Guthrie, Doug. (2013). Corporate Universities: An Emerging Threat to Graduate Business Education. *Forbes*, 01/22/2013.

4. A few concepts adapted from Birdi, K., Allan, C., & Warr, P. (1997). Correlates and Perceived Outcomes of Four Types of Employee Development Activity. *Journal of Applied Psychology, 82*(6), 845–857.

5. Azulay, H. (2013). Learning Beyond the Comfort Zone. [Article]. *T+D, 67*(1), 76–77.

6. Brown, M. (2008). Comfort Zone: Model or Metaphor? (Undetermined). [Article]. *Australian Journal of Outdoor Education, 12*(1), 3–12.

7. Dragoni, L., Tesluk, P. E., Russell, J. E. A., & Oh, I.-S. (2009). Understanding Managerial Development: Integrating Developmental Assignments, Learning Orientation, and Access to Developmental Opportunities in Predicting Managerial Competencies. *Academy of Management Journal, 52*(4), 731–743; McCauley, C. D., Ruderman, M. N., Ohlott, P. J., & Morrow, J. E. (1994). Assessing the Developmental Components of Managerial Jobs. *Journal of Applied Psychology, 79*, 544–560; McCall, M. W, Lombardo, M. M., & Morrison, A. M. (1988). The Lessons of Experience: How Successful Executives Develop on the Job. Lexington, Mass.: Lexington Books.

8. See the Developmental Challenge Profile in McCauley, C. D., Ruderman, M. N., Ohlott, P. J., & Morrow, J. E. (1994). Assessing the Developmental Components of Managerial Jobs. *Journal of Applied Psychology, 79*, 544–560.

9. Ibid.

10. Marques, J. (2012). The Dynamics of Accelerated Learning. *Business Education & Accreditation, 4*(1), 101–112; Lucas, B.

(2005). The Science Behind Accelerated Learning. *Training Journal*, 33–36, 34.

11. Caligiuri, P., & Tarique, I. (2009). Predicting Effectiveness in Global Leadership Activities. *Journal of World Business, 44*(3), 336; Dragoni, L., Tesluk, P. E., Russell, J. E. A., & Oh, I.-S. (2009). Understanding Managerial Development: Integrating Developmental Assignments, Learning Orientation, and Access to Developmental Opportunities in Predicting Managerial Competencies. *Academy of Management Journal, 52*(4), 731–743; Hannah, S. T., & Avolio, B. J. (2010). Ready or Not: How Do We Accelerate the Developmental Readiness of Leaders? *Journal of Organizational Behavior, 31*(8), 1181.

12. McKeon, K. J. (1995). What Is This Thing Called Accelerated Learning? *Training & Development, 49*(6), 64.

13. Ibid; also see Steinhouse, R. (2011). Hidden Barriers to Learning and How to Overcome Them. *Training & Management Development Methods, 25*(1), 401–406.

14. Brown, M. (2008). Comfort Zone: Model or Metaphor. *Australian Journal of Outdoor Education, 12*(1), 3–12.

15. DeRue, D. S., & Wellman, N. (2009). Developing Leaders via Experience: The Role of Developmental Challenge, Learning Orientation, and Feedback Availability. *Journal of Applied Psychology, 94*(4), 859.

16. Dragoni, L., Tesluk, P. E., Russell, J. E. A., & Oh, In-Sue (2009). Understanding Managerial Development: Integrating Developmental Assignments, Learning Orientation, and Access to Developmental Opportunities in Predicting Managerial Competencies. *Academy of Management Journal, 52*(4), 731–743.

17. Margolies, Mike (2013). Out of Our Comfort Zones. The SportINMind. http://www.thesportinmind.com/articles/out-of-our-comfort-zones/.

18. Karaevli, Ayse, & Hall, Douglas. (2006). How Career Variety Promotes the Adaptability of Managers: A Theoretical Model.

Journal of Vocational Behavior, 69(2006), 359–373.; McCauley, C. D., Eastman, L. J., & Ohlott, P. J. (1995). Linking Management Selection and Development through Stretch Assignments. *Human Resource Management, 34*(1), 93–115.

19. These are based on Macaux, W. P. (2010). Making the Most of Stretch Assignments. [Article]. *T+D, 64*(6), 48-53; McCauley, C. D., Eastman, L. J., & Ohlott, P. J. (1995). Linking Management Selection and Development through Stretch Assignments. *Human Resource Management, 34*(1), 93–115; Salopek, J. J. (2007). Stretching: Good for Mind and Body. [Article]. *T+D, 61*(10), 18–20.

20. Lombardo, M. M., & Eichinger, R. W. (2000). High Potentials as High Learners. *Human Resource Management, 39,* 321–330.

21. Eichinger, R. W., & Lombardo, M. M. (2004). Learning Agility as a Prime Indicator of Potential. *Human Resource Planning, 27*(4), 12–16.

22. Lombardo, M. M., & Eichinger, R. W. (2000). High Potentials as High Learners. *Human Resource Management, 39,* 321–330.

23. Mitchinson, A., & Morris, Robert. (2012). Learning About Learning Agility. Center for Creative Leadership.

24. Derue, Scott, Ashford, Susan, & Myers, Christopher. Learning Agility: In Search of Conceptual Clarity and Theoretical Grounding. *Industrial and Organizational Psychology, 5,* 258–279.

25. Dai, G., De Meuse, K. P., & Tang, K. Y. (2013). The Role of Learning Agility in Executive Career Success: The Results of Two Field Studies. *Journal of Managerial Issues, 25*(2), 108–131,105.

26. Cavanaugh, Caitlin, & Zelin, Alexandra. (2012). Learning Agility. A Hot Topics Paper. Prepared by the Visibility Committee of the Society for Industrial and Organizational Psychology.

27. Dries, N., Vantilborgh, T., & Pepermans, R. (2012). The Role of Learning Agility and Career Variety in the Identification and Development of High Potential Employees. *Personnel Review, 41*(3), 340–358. doi: http://dx.doi.org/10.1108/00483481211212977.

28. Swisher, V. (2013). Learning Agility: The "X" Factor in Identifying and Developing Future Leaders. *Industrial and Commercial Training, 45*(3), 139–142. doi: http://dx.doi.org/10.1108/00197851311320540.

29. Dai, G., De Meuse, K. P., & Tang, K. Y. (2013). The Role of Learning Agility in Executive Career Success: The Results of Two Field Studies. *Journal of Managerial Issues, 25*(2), 108–131,105.

30. De Meuse, K. P., Dai, G., Hallenbeck, G., & Tang, K. (2008). Global Talent Management: Using Learning Agility to Identify High Potentials Around the World. Los Angeles, CA: Korn/Ferry International.

31. Connor, J. (2011). Deepening the Talent Pool through Learning Agility. *People Management, 40.*

32. My interpretation is heavily influenced by the work of Paula Caligiuri on cultural agility. See Caligiuri, P. (2013). Developing culturally agile global business leaders. Organizational Dynamics, 42, 175–182; Caligiuri, P. (2012). Cultural Agility: Building a Pipeline of Globally Successful Professionals. Jossey-Bass Publishing.

Chapter 10

1. For a thorough discussion on expertise and its origin, see Chi, M. T. H., Glaser, R., & Farr, M. (1988). *The Nature of Expertise*. Hillsdale, NJ: Erlbaum.

2. Salas, E., & Rosen, M. A. (2010). Experts at Work: Principles for Developing Expertise in Organizations. In Kozlowski, S. W. J., & Salas, E. (Eds.). *Learning, Training, and*

Development in Organizations (pp. 99–134). New York: Routledge; Ericsson, K. A., Prietula, M. J., & Cokely, E. T. (2007, Jul). The Making of an Expert. *Harvard Business Review, 85,* 114–121.

3. Ericsson, K. A., Prietula, M. J., & Cokely, E. T. (2007, Jul). The Making of an Expert. *Harvard Business Review, 85,* 114–121.

4. Ibid.

5. Bransford, J., Brown, A., & Cocking, R. (1999). How People Learn: Brain, Mind, Experience, and School. Committee on Developments in the Science of Learning, National Research Council.

6. Salas, E., & Rosen, M. A. (2010). Experts at Work: Principles Developing Expertise in Organizations. In Kozlowski, S. W. J., & Salas, E. (Eds.). *Learning, Training, and Development in Organizations* (pp. 99–134). New York: Routledge.

7. Dreyfus, S. E. (2004). The Five-Stage Model of Adult Skill Acquisition. *Bulletin of Science, Technology & Society, 24*(3), 177–181; Dreyfus, H. L., & Dreyfus, S. E. (1986). *Mind over Machine: The Power of Human Intuition and Expertise in the Age of the Computer.* Oxford: Basil Blackwell; Cornford, I., & Athanasou, J. (1995). Developing Expertise through Training. *Industrial and Commercial Training, 27*(2), 10.

8. Ericsson, K. A., Prietula, M. J., & Cokely, E. T. (2007, Jul). The Making of an Expert. *Harvard Business Review, 85,* 114–121.

9. Ibid.

10. Ibid.

11. Salas, E., & Rosen, M. A. (2010). Experts at Work: Principles Developing Expertise in Organizations. In Kozlowski, S. W. J., & Salas, E. (Eds.). *Learning, Training, and Development in Organizations* (pp. 99–134). New York: Routledge.

12. Ibid.

13. Ibid.

14. Ibid.

15. Goldman, Ellen. (2006). Strategic Thinking at the Top: What Matters in Developing Expertise. Academy of Management Best Conference paper.

16. Ibid.

17. Mauboussin, M. J. (2008, 02). What Good Are Experts. *Harvard Business Review, 86*, 43–44.

18. AMA 2012 Critical Skills Survey. American Management Association. www.amanet.org.

19. Ibid.

20. Ibid.

21. Ibid.

22. Bodell, Lisa. (2012). Work Skills You'll Need to Survive the "Conceptual Age". CNN.com; Bodel, Lisa. (2012). *Kill the Company: End the Status Quo, Start an Innovation Revolution*. Brookline, Mass: Bibliomotion.

23. Ibid.

24. Caligiuri, Paula. (2012). *Cultural Agility: Building a Pipeline of Successful Global Professionals*. San Francisco, CA: Jossey-Bass.

25. Passion, V. (2012). They're Experts, But Can They Be Trainers? *T + D, 66*(2), 54–58, 8.

26. Ibid.

27. How to use subject matter experts. (2007). e.learning age, 25.

28. Passion, V. (2012). They're Experts, But Can They Be Trainers? *T + D, 66*(2), 54–58, 8.

29. Lee, Kendra. (2008). Leverage Subject Matter Experts. *Training, Mar/Apr, 45*: 18.

Chapter 11

1. Briscoe, D. R., Schuler, R. S., & Tarique, I. (2012). *International Human Resource Management: Policies and Practices for Multinational Enterprises* (4th ed.). New York: Routledge.

2. Ibid.

3. Ibid.

4. Porter, M. E. (1980). *Competitive Strategy: Techniques for Analyzing Industries and Competitors*. New York: Free Press.

5. Developing Results. Aligning Learning Goals and Outcomes with Business Performance Measures, Whitepaper, Vol. 3, No. 5, 2012.

6. Becker, B., Beatty, D., & Huselid, M. (2009). *Differentiated Workforce: Transforming Talent into Strategic Impact.* Boston, Mass.: Harvard Business School Press Books.

7. Huselid, M. A., Beatty, R. W., & Becker, B. E. (2006). "A Players" or "A Positions"?: The Strategic Logic of Workforce Management. *Harvard Business Review, 84,* 143–144.

8. Tarique, I., & Schuler, R. (2012). Global Talent Management Literature Review. A report prepared from SHRM Foundation.

9. Friedman, B. A. (2009). Human Resource Management Role: Implications for Corporate Reputation. *Corporate Reputation Review, 12*(3), 229–244; Wayne, J. H., & Casper, W. J. (2012). Why Does Firm Reputation in Human Resource Policies Influence College Students? The Mechanisms Underlying Job Pursuit Intentions. *Human Resource Management, 51*(1), 121–142.

10. Tarique, I., & Schuler, R. S. (2010). Global Talent Management: Literature Review, Integrative Framework, and Suggestions for Further Research. *Journal of World Business, 45*(2), 122.

11. Tarique, I., & Schuler, R. (2014). Typology of Talent Management Strategies. In Sparrow, Paul, Scullion, Hugh, & Tarique, Ibraiz. (Eds.). Strategic Talent Management: Contemporary Issues in International Context. New York: Cambridge University Press.

12. McDonnell, A. (2011). Still Fighting the "War for Talent"? Bridging the Science Versus Practice Gap. *Journal of Business and Psychology, 26*(2), 169–173.

13. Allen, J., & de Grip, A. (2012). Does Skill Obsolescence Increase the Risk of Employment Loss? *Applied Economics, 44*(25), 3237–3245.

14. Tarique, I., & Schuler, R. S. (2010). Global Talent Management: Literature Review, Integrative Framework, and Suggestions for Further Research. *Journal of World Business, 45*(2), 122; Tarique, I., & Schuler, R. (2012). Global Talent Management Literature Review. A report prepared from SHRM Foundation; Tarique, I., & Weisbord, E. (2013). Antecedents of Dynamic Cross-Cultural Competence in Adult Third Culture Kids (ATCKs). *Journal of Global Mobility, 2*, 1.

15. Caligiuri, P., Lazarova, M., & Tarique, I., (2005). Training, Learning, and Development in Multinational Corporations. In Scullion, H., & Linehan, M. (Eds.). *International Human Resource Management*. New York: Palgrave Macmillan.

16. Ibid.

17. Caligiuri, P. M. (2006). Performance Measurement in a Cross-National Context: Evaluating the Success of Global Assignments. In Bennett, W., Woehr, D., & Lance, C. (Eds.). *Performance Measurement: Current Perspectives and Future Challenges*. Mahwah: Lawrence Erlbaum Associates, Inc. Publishers.

18. Kealey, Daniel J., & Protheroe, David R. (1996). The Effectiveness of Cross-Cultural Training for Expatriates: An Assessment of the Literature on the Issue. *International Journal of Intercultural Relations, 20*, 141–165; Tarique, I., & Caligiuri, P. (2004). Training and Development of International Staff. In

Harzing, Anne-Wil, & Van Ruysseveldt, Joris (Eds.). *International Human Resource Management*. London: Sage.

19. Selmer, Jan, Torbiorn, Ingemar, & de Leon, Corinna T. (1998). Sequential Cross-Cultural Training for Expatriate Business Managers: Pre-departure and Post-arrival. *International Journal of Human Resource Management, 9*, 831–840.

20. Kealey, Daniel J., & Protheroe, David R. (1996). The Effectiveness of Cross-Cultural Training for Expatriates: An Assessment of the Literature on the Issue. *International Journal of Intercultural Relations, 20*, 141–165.

21. Tarique, I., & Weisbord, E. (2013). Antecedents of Dynamic Cross-Cultural Competence in Adult Third Culture Kids (ATCKs), *Journal of Global Mobility, 2*, 1; Bonebright, D. A. (2010). Adult Third Culture Kids: HRD Challenges and Opportunities. *Human Resource Development International, 13*, 351-359.

22. Beechler, S., & Javidan, M. (2007). Leading with a Global Mindset. In Javidan, M., Hitt, M. A., & Steers, R. M. (Eds.). Advances in International Management. Vol. 19 (pp.131–170). The Global Mindset. Oxford, UK: JAI Press/Elsevier.

23. Noe, R. A. (2008). *Employee Training and Development* (4th ed.). New York: McGraw-Hill/Irwin.

24. Ibid.

25. The Value of Evaluation: Making Training Evaluation More Effective. (2009). An ASTD Research Study.

26. Kraiger, K., Ford, J., & Salas, E. (1993). Application of Cognitive, Skill-Based, and Affective Theories of Learning Outcomes to New Methods of Training Evaluation. *Journal of Applied Psychology, 78*, 211–228; Collins D. (2002). Performance-Level Evaluation Methods Used in Management Development Studies from 1986 to 2000. *Human Resource Development Review, 1*, 91-110; Swanson, R., & Holton, E. (1999). *Results: How to Assess Performance, Learning,*

and Perceptions in Organizations. San Francisco, CA: Berrett-Koehler.

27. Kirkpatrick, Donald. (2010). How to Apply Kirkpatrick's Four Levels of Evaluation. *T+D, December,* 38–39.

28. Baldwin, T. T., & Ford, J. K. (1988). Transfer of Training: A Review and Directions for Future Research. *Personnel Psychology, 41,* 63-105; Wexley, K. N., & Latham, G. P. (2002). *Developing and Training Human Resources in Organizations* (3rd ed.). Upper Saddle River, NJ: Prentice Hall.

29. Kraiger, K., Ford, J., & Salas, E. (1993). Application of Cognitive, Skill-Based, and Affective Theories of Learning Outcomes to New Methods of Training Evaluation. *Journal of Applied Psychology, 78,* 211–228.

30. Phillips, J. J. (1996). How Much Is the Training Worth? *Training & Development, 50*(4), 20; Phillips, J. J. (1996). ROI: The Search for Best Practices. *Training & Development, 50*(2), 42.

31. See Campbell, D. T., Stanley, J. C., & Gage, N. L. (1981). *Experimental and Quasi-Experimental Designs for Research.* Boston, Mass.: Houghton Mifflin; Keppel, G. (1991). *Design and Analysis. A Researcher's Handbook.* Upper Saddle River, NJ: Prentice Hall.

Chapter 12

1. Future Work Skills 2020. Institute for the Future for the University of Phoenix Research Institute. www.iftf.org.

2. 21st Century Skills and the Workplace. A 2013 Microsoft Partners in Learning and Pearson Foundation Study, May 28, 2013. http://www.gallup.com.

3. Based on comments from Richard Florida in Florida, Richard, Gardner, Howard, Gladwell, Malcon, Ferriss, Tim, Rath, Tom, Tichy, Noel, Ericson, Tamara, & Penn, Mark. (2007). The Future of Learning and Work. *T+D, December.*

4. Based on comments from Mark Penn in Florida, Richard, Gardner, Howard, Gladwell, Malcon, Ferriss, Tim, Rath, Tom, Tichy, Noel, Ericson, Tamara, & Penn, Mark. (2007). The Future of Learning and Work. *T+D, December.*

5. Based on comments from Malcolm Gladwell in Florida, Richard, Gardner, Howard, Gladwell, Malcon, Ferriss, Tim, Rath, Tom, Tichy, Noel, Ericson, Tamara, & Penn, Mark. (2007). The Future of Learning and Work. *T+D, December.*

6. Marsh, G. (2012). Soft Skills and the Future. *Training Journal,* 39–41, February.

7. Ibid.

8. Ibid.

9. Ibid.

10. Ibid.

11. Ibid.

12. Ibid.

13. Williams, W. (2011). Employee Competencies for the Future. *Journal of Corporate Recruiting Leadership,* 6(4), 15–17.

14. Ibid.

15. Ibid.

16. Ibid.

17. For more information on this topic, see Hoch, J. E., & Kozlowski, S. J. (2012). Leading Virtual Teams: Hierarchical Leadership, Structural Supports, and Shared Team Leadership. *Journal of Applied Psychology,* doi:10.1037/a0030264; Hardaker, M., & Ward, B. K. (1987). How to Make a Team Work. *Harvard Business Review,* 65(6), 112–119; Kimble, C. (2011). Building Effective Virtual Teams: How to Overcome the Problems of Trust and Identity in Virtual Teams. *Global Business & Organizational Excellence,* 30(2), 6–15; Mankins, M., Bird, A., & Root, J. (2013). Making Star Teams Out of Star Players. *Harvard Business Review,* 91(1), 74–78.

18. For more information on this topic, see Head, A. J., Van Hoeck, M., Eschler, J., & Fullerton, S. (2013). What Information Competencies Matter in Today's Workplace? *Library & Information Research, 37*(114), 74–104; Gleick, J. (2011). Drowning, Surfing and Surviving. *New Scientist, 210*(2806), 30-31; Hargittai, E., Neuman, W., & Curry, O. (2011). Overwhelmed and Underinformed? How Americans Keep Up with Current Events in the Age of Social Media. Conference Papers—International Communication Association, 1–27; Coping with Information Overload. (2012). *Managing Information, 18*(10), 24–27.

19. For more information on this topic, see Caligiuri, P., & Lazarova, M. (2002). A Model for the Influence of Social Interaction and Social Support on Female Expatriates' Cross-Cultural Adjustment. *International Journal of Human Resource Management, 13*(5), 761–772; Githens, R. P. (2006). Cautions: Implementing Interpersonal Interaction in Workplace E-Learning. *Techtrends: Linking Research and Practice to Improve Learning, 50*(5), 21–27.

20. For more information on this topic, see Jones, Rodney, & Hafner, Christoph A. (2012). *Understanding Digital Literacies: A Practical Introduction*. New York: Routledge; Stripling, B. (2010). Teaching Students to Think in the Digital Environment: Digital Literacy and Digital Inquiry. *School Library Monthly, 26*(8), 16–19; Tan, E. (2013). Informal Learning on YouTube: Exploring Digital Literacy in Independent Online Learning. *Learning, Media and Technology, 38*(4), 463–477; Meyers, E. M., Erickson, I., & Small, R. V. (2013). Digital Literacy and Informal Learning Environments: An Introduction. *Learning, Media and Technology, 38*(4), 355–367; Crush, P. (2011). Filling the Digital Skills Gap. *Marketing* (00253650), 33–34.

21. Noe, R. (2001). *Employee Training and Development*. Boston, Mass.: McGraw-Hill.

22. Ferdman, B., & Broady, S. (1996). Models of Diversity Training. In Landis, D., & Bhagat, R. S. (Eds.). *Handbook of Intercultural Training* (2nd ed.) (pp. 282–303). Thousand Oaks, CA: Sage.

23. De León, Diego S., LaVelle, Katherine, & Cantrell, Susan M. (2013). Trends Reshaping the Future of HR Tapping Skills Anywhere, Anytime. Accenture, Institute for High Performance.

24. Gartside, David, Silverstone, Yaarit, Farley, Catherine, & Cantrell, Susan M. (2013). Trends Reshaping the Future of HR. The Rise of the Extended Workforce. Accenture, Institute for High Performance.

25. Ibid.

26. Future Work Skills 2020. Institute for the Future for the University of Phoenix Research Institute. www.iftf.org.

27. Rothwell, William. (2010). The Future of Succession Planning, *T+D, September*.

28. Hird, Martin, & Sparrow, Paul. (2012). Learning & Development: Seeking a Renewed Focus. Whitepaper, Center for Performance Led HR.

29. Frefeld, Lorri. (2012). The Future of Training Is Already Here. *Training,* November 5: http://www.trainingmag.com/content/future-training-already-here.

30. See Mattox, John. (2012). Measuring the Effectiveness of Informal Learning Methodologies. *T+D, February*; Weinstein, Margery. (2013). Regulate Informal Learning. *Training*. www.trainingmag.com; Wisniewski, Brenda, & McMahon, Kevin. (2005). Formalizing Informal Learning. *Chief Learning Officer, 3/29/05*.

31. Ibid.

32. See Caligiuri, P., & Tarique, I. (2009). Predicting Effectiveness in Global Leadership Activities. *Journal of World Business, 44*(3), 336.

33. See Schmidt, A. M., & Ford, J. K. (2003). Learning within a Learner Control Training Environment: The Interactive

Effects of Goal Orientation and Metacognitive Instruction on Learning Outcomes. *Personnel Psychology, 56*(2), 405; Guthrie, C. (2010). Towards Greater Learner Control: Web Supported Project-Based Learning. *Journal of Information Systems Education, 21*(1), 121–130.

34. See Knese, William F, CMA, C.F.M., C.P.A. (2013). A Commitment to Continuous Learning. *Strategic Finance, 95*(6), 6 6, 61; Kuznia, K. D., Kerno, Steven J., Jr., & Gilley, A. (2010). The Correlates and Influences of Career-Related Continuous Learning: Implications for Management Professionals. *Performance Improvement Quarterly, 22*(4), 7; Bonnie, D. C. (2009). Manufacturing Plant as Classroom: Reinventing Continuous Learning. *Plant Engineering, 63*(3), 10.

35. See Wright, K. (2013). Be a Lifelong Learner. *Training*. Retrieved from http://www.trainingmag.com/content/be-life-long-learner; Maurer, T. J., & Weiss, E. M. (2010). Continuous Learning Skill Demands: Associations with Managerial Job Content, Age, and Experience. *Journal of Business and Psychology, 25*(1), 1 13. doi: 10.1007/s10869-009-9126-0; Sessa, V. I., & London, M. (2005). *Continuous Learning in Organizations: Individual, Group, and Organizational Perspectives*. Mahwah, NJ: Lawrence Erlbaum; Molloy, J. C., & Noe, R. A. (2010). "Learning" a Living: Continuous Learning for Survival in Today's Talent Market. In Kozlowski, S. W. J., & Salas, E. (Eds.). *Learning, Training, and Development in Organizations* (pp. 333–361). New York: Routledge/Taylor & Francis Group.

36. See Leonard, B. (2011). Managing Virtual Teams. *HR Magazine, 56*(6), 39–42; Dobson, S. (2011). Virtual Teams Expected to Grow: Survey. *Canadian HR Reporter, 24*(17), 3.

37. Brett, J., Behfar, K., & Kern, M. C. (2006, 11). Managing Multicultural Teams. *Harvard Business Review, 84*, 84–91; Cheng, C., Chua, R. Y. J., Morris, M. W., & Lee, L. (2012). Finding the Right Mix: How the Composition of Self-Managing

Multicultural Teams' Cultural Value Orientation Influences Performance over Time. *Journal of Organizational Behavior, 33*(3), 389; Gupta, S. (2008). Mine the Potential of Multicultural Teams. *HR Magazine, 53*(10), 79–80, 82, 84.

38. See Stahl, G., Björkman, I., Farndale, E., Morris, S., Paauwe, J., & Stiles, P. (2012). Six Principles of Effective Global Talent Management. *MIT Sloan Management Review, 53*(2), 25 32;Tarique, I., & Schuler, R. S. (2010). Global Talent Management: Literature Review, Integrative Framework, and Suggestions for Further Research. [Article]. *Journal of World Business, 45*(2), 122 133. doi: 10.1016/j.jwb.2009.09.019.

39. Bodell, Lisa. (2011). Thinking about the Future of Learning, Learning 2020. *TrainingIndustry Quarterly,* Winter 2011.

40. Becker, B. E., Huselid, M. A., & Beatty, R. W. (2009). *The Differentiated Workforce: Transforming Talent into Strategic Impact.* Boston, Mass.: Harvard Business Press.

Index